Tamaracks:
Canadian Poetry
for the
21st Century

Edited by James Deahl

LUMMOX Press
San Pedro, California
2018

©2018 LUMMOX Press

Cover art by Debbie Okun Hill

All rights revert to the contributors upon publication.
All rights reserved. No part of this book can be reproduced without the express written permission of the author, except in the case of written reviews.

ISBN 978-0-9997784-2-5

Library of Congress Control Number: 2018949369

First edition

PO Box 5301
San Pedro, CA 90733
www.lummoxpress.com

Printed in the United States of America

Mission Statement:

   The LUMMOX Press was established in 1994 and has published the Little Red Book series and the LUMMOX Journal. It publishes chapbooks, a perfect bound book series, the LUMMOX Poetry Anthology & Contest (annually), and "e-copies" (PDFs) of many of the perfect bound titles. Over the past 24 years over 150 titles have been published.

   The goal of the press is to elevate the bar for poetry, while bringing the "word" to an international audience. I am proud to offer this book as part of that effort.

   For more information and to see our growing catalog of choices, please go to *www.lummoxpress.com*

While it is not the privilege of an editor to dedicate an anthology,
I am confident that most, if not all, of the present contributors
will join me in dedicating *Tamaracks* to the memory of Milton Acorn,
Raymond Souster, Simcha (Sam) Simchovitch, Dorothy Livesay,
and Al Purdy — true friends, true Canadians, and true poets.

— James Deahl

CONTENTS

Editor's Introduction i

Robert S. Acorn
    Bedspread 1
    Passchendaele 1

Sylvia Adams
    No Pictures of Him Smiling 2

Becky D. Alexander
    Buried Deep 4

Donna Allard
    map 5

Rosemary Aubert
    Made In China 6
    The Plague 1665 - 1666 6

Henry Beissel
    4 from: Stones to Harvest 7
    Manifesto in Times of War 9
    Amaryllis 10

Nancy M. Bell
    Henge 12

Sharon Berg
    Prophesy 13

Steven Michael Berzensky (Mick Burrs)
    Breathing In the Bees 15
    Notes on Mandelstam 16
    Heart 16

Clara Blackwood
    Persephone Unbound 17

Robert A. Boates
    Late September 18
    The Good Life 18

Kent Bowman
    Vacancy at the Blues Barbershop (Chicago) 19

Frances Boyle
    Pelican Narrows 20

Mary Lee Bragg
    My Mother's Birds 21

Allan Briesmaster
    To Du Fu, after 13 Centuries 22
    In Flight 22

Ronnie R. Brown
    For Keeps 23
    Thoughts After The Carnage 24
    An Object Believed to be Human Remains 25

April Bulmer
    Buffalograss Jail 26
    Skins 26
Rebecca Clifford
    Turkey Vultures 27
Patrick Connors
    Exit Poll 28
Tony Cosier
    Saw Music 29
    Stone Steps 30
Lorna Crozier
    The Mask 31
    Time Studies 32
    My Last Erotic Poem 33
    The Underworld 34
Phillip Crymble
    Nursery 35
Robert Currie
    Thief 36
    Because I Never 37
David Day
    Just Say 'No' to Family Values 38
James Deahl
    Ulysses 41
    Confronting The Idea Of The Good On A Rainy Night In Early May 42
    Silence In The Fields Of Autumn 43
Stewart Donovan
    In Memory of Seamus Heaney, 1939-2013 44
    The Sea Air at Middlehead 45
G. W. Down
    Trolling Toward Terror 46
Gertrude Olga Down
    Babelplatz, Berlin 47
Jennifer Lynn Dunlop
    Blue Delphiniums 48
Bernadette Gabay Dyer
    In the Aftermath 49
    Where Sunlight Dare Not Follow 50
Margaret Patricia Eaton
    Sunflowers 51
    Winter Woods 51
Ronda Wicks Eller
    Prostrate in Byzantium 52

CONTENTS (continued)

Daniela Elza
    autobiography of grief 1 53
Joseph A. Farina
    morning essence 54
Venera Fazio
    Broken 55
    Point of Departure, 1951 56
Fran Figge
    The Fault of the Apple 57
Doris Fiszer
    In the Year Before She Died... 58
    Foraging 58
Kate Marshall Flaherty
    Lost 60
Jennifer L. Foster
    Wild Apple Tree 61
    In Snug Harbour, Georgian Bay 61
Linda Frank
    A Long Time Coming... 62
    Chasing Shadows 63
    You've Been On My Mind 64
Ryan Gibbs
    Daylight my Darknesses 65
Sharon Goodier
    Nothing Left Behind 66
Katherine L. Gordon
    Leonardo's Flying Machine 67
    Beowulf's Blade 67
Elizabeth Greene
    Reading Ivy Compton-Burnett 68
Andreas Gripp
    The West Coast of Somewhere 69
    Marooning the Muse 69
Richard M. Grove
    Aching to be On the Water, March 22 70
David Haskins
    Resilience 71
    Reclamation... 73
Rhoda Hassmann
    Bronze-Skinned Woman 74
    Between Massacres 74
Debbie Okun Hill
    An Old Miner's House 75

Eryn Hiscock
    Harem (Ted Bundy Poem) 76
    After *Frankenstein* 76

Lawrence Hopperton
    McCraney 77

Laurence Hutchman
    La Dentellière 79
    Milkweed 80

Luciano Iacobelli
    The Egg Poem 81

Keith Inman
    Glass 82
    Lake Fever 83

Susan Ioannou
    Mineralogy Lesson 84
    Imagine That Greek Island 84

I.B. Iskov
    When He Died, He Took One Last Poem with Him 85

Ellen S. Jaffe
    Water Children 86
    Another Kind of War Story 87

Carol Keller
    Dirty Love 88

Eva Kolacz
    Inquiry into Pastoral Life 89

Maureen Korp
    Friday afternoon 90

Laurie Kruk
    Birds of America 91

Donna Langevin
    In the Café du Monde 93
    If "Live Oaks" Could Laugh 94

Ruth Latta
    "Poetry Café" at a Retirement Residence 95

Beth Learn
    Bethie at the Beach 96

John B. Lee
    Bringing the Farmhouse Down 99
    The Ungoable 100
    On kindness 102

Bernice Lever
    Young Eyes Ask Why 104

Norma West Linder
    Little Boy Lost 105
    Last Poem for Irving Layton 105
Annick MacAskill
    Tatiana in Gaspra, 1902 106
Carol Malyon
    the morgue attendant & his wife... 107
Blaine Marchand
    In the White Giant's Thigh 108
    Life is a Train 109
    Zakat 110
    Song of Little Squirrel 111
Steven McCabe
    Lament of A Fool in the Tradition of Sacrifice, Folly, and Clairvoyance 112
Elizabeth McCallister
    Noticing the Scenery 114
Mori McCrae
    Gravity 115
Ian McCulloch
    Poppa 116
    Carl Martin's Tongue Stuck To The Merry-Go-Round 118
Susan McMaster
    Sign of Respect 119
    How God sees 119
Bronwen McRae
    At the A & W 120
    Going Back 121
Rhonda Melanson
    Strong Women... 122
    One Catholic's Apology for Residential Schools 122
Bruce Meyer
    My Father's Passing Contained No Poetry 123
    The Death of Christianity in Oil City 125
    Two Students on the College Lawn 126
Michael Mirolla
    To a poet struggling to recover her words 127
    The Bear 128
Lynda Monahan
    taken away 129
A.F. Moritz
    Baltimore May 2015.. 130
    Philosopher and Southern Ohio 131
    Names of Birds.. 132

Deborah A. Morrison
    Crystal Beach 133
Colin Morton
    Last Rites 134
Marion Mutala
    Seductress 136
Lois Nantais
    A Prayer to the Wild 137
Shane Neilson
    Angelic Salutation 138
Diane Attwell Palfrey
    Before and After 140
Brian Palmu
    Canron Steel 141
Deborah Panko
    Hummingbird 142
Chris Pannell
    Water Lilies 143
    A Day Trip to El Alamein 145
Gianna Patriarca
    Italian Women 146
    Returning 146
Nolan Natasha Pike
    Forks of the Credit River 147
Stella Mazur Preda
    The Tolling of the Bell 148
Robert Priest
    Poem for a Tall Woman.. 149
Brian Purdy
    'basturd injuns' 150
Kathy Robertson
    Lest We Forget 151
Denis Robillard
    The Body Sublime 152
Kate Rogers
    In the Dark, Age Eight after My Screams Wake Me 153
Linda Rogers
    Crow Revival, Second Line Beatitudes 154
    A Blessing 154
Karen Shenfeld
    Woman at the River, Washing.. 155
    Weatherman 156
    Milestones 157

Glen Sorestad
- Blue Crabs, Galveston Bay ... 158
- Banana Loaf and Two Small Oranges ... 159
- A Straightener of Nails ... 159

Ken Stange
- Learn To Appreciate Doors ... 160

J.J. Steinfeld
- Where You Get Lost or Go Astray ... 162

Dane Swan
- From these eyes ... 163
- Blackface ... 164

Lynn Tait
- Slipstream ... 165
- Fishing in South-east Ontario ... 166

Jennifer Tan
- Still ... 167
- The Wind Chime ... 168

Grace Vermeer
- Returning To Fairpoint, Ohio ... 169
- The Monks of Skellig Michael ... 172
- Ghazal For Eve's Daughters ... 173
- One Cup Holds Twenty Thousand Small Wonders ... 174

Wendy Visser
- News Flash ... 175
- Fish Fry ... 175

Bruce Whiteman
- Slightly Below Normal ... 176

Elana Wolff
- Messenger Suite ... 177

Jan Wood
- Shafts of Sun ... 181

Ed Woods
- Alzheimer's Lack of Compassion ... 182

Anna Yin
- My Body Is a Flute ... 183

Acknowledgements ... 184

Contributors ... 193

INTRODUCTION

TAMARACKS HAS BEEN EDITED to achieve two chief goals: to present readers with some fine poetry and to show where Canadian poetry stands about one fifth of the way into the 21st century. And, of course, with this collection I wish to make a statement concerning Canadian poetry and to introduce our poetry to readers outside Canada, especially in the United States. In addition, I feel it's essential to provide both critic and academic with as comprehensive and reliable a target as possible. Therefore, *all* Canadian poets were invited to submit their best work. I contacted The Writers' Union of Canada and The League of Canadian Poets as well as each of our provincial writers' organizations to insure their members were aware of my call for submissions. I also individually invited well over one hundred Canadian poets who are my personal friends and/or colleagues.

Unfortunately, there are some very good poets who, for a variety of reasons, elected not to participate in this project. I fully respect and support their choice. Sadly, a few publishers refused permission to use poetry over which they hold reprint rights. At least one poet was excluded for this reason. (I am much less happy and supportive about this.) But such is always the case with collections of this nature. The 113 poets included here are the poets who want, and most importantly, whose poetry *deserves*, to be here, and that is what counts.

I wish to stress, however, that this anthology is not about poets. It is solely about poems. While *Tamaracks* is national in scope, containing the work of poets from Halifax (Brian Purdy) to Victoria (Linda Rogers), I have paid no attention to a poet's place of birth or regional location. Nor do I care about a poet's ethnicity, gender, race, or reputation. Having won the Governor General's Award for Poetry or the Milton Acorn Memorial People's Poetry Award is no guarantee of acceptance. While it is wonderful to have published in leading journals like *Queen's Quarterly* and the *Dalhousie Review*, I only judge the poems that have been submitted for consideration, never where they were previously published. Poets and reputations are neither accepted nor rejected, only poems are.

While I have chosen each of the following poems, poets were asked to select six pieces to represent their finest work. Thus, each poet had to decide which poems best illustrated the body of his or her poetry: a most invidious burden. But I requested the poets to do exactly that, and I knew it would not be easy because many of the following contributors have published several full-sized and widely celebrated collections over a period of decades. One cannot underestimate the difficulty of selecting from an entire lifetime's work. But it was important to me to allow each poet to put his or her best foot forward.

There are many types of poetry written in Canada, and I hope you will find them here. Our legacy of People's Poetry, dating from the Confederation Poets of the late 19th century, has survived into the new century, as have such 20th century movements as Modernism, Confessional Poetry, and Post-Modernism. Formalism has renewed itself, and has its champions, too. Regional voices are, perhaps, stronger than ever. As a reader, I have my likes and dislikes. Nonetheless, I have attempted to show the full spectrum of our poetry. *Tamaracks* gives an indication of where Canadian poetry finds itself in 2018 and there is a hint of its possible future directions. As to my personal likes and dislikes, which the reader has a right to know, my devotion to poetry started over half a century ago during the winter of 1963-'64, and my early heroes were Carl Sandburg (*Honey and Salt*) and Allen Ginsberg (*Howl and Other Poems*). They remain major heroes, but I have absorbed many other influences, initially from English-language literature, and a bit later from world literature.

In terms of Canadian poetry, I quickly gravitated toward the work of Milton Acorn, Dorothy Livesay, and Raymond Souster. Acorn, Livesay, Souster, Al Purdy, and Sam Simchovitch soon became lasting friends, as have many of the poets whose work is to be found in the present volume, such as John B. Lee, Ronnie R. Brown, and Bruce Meyer. Thus, my roots are in Populist/People's Poetry, but I have never been limited to that or any other school. Indeed, my admiration for the poetry of Robert Lowell and Richard Wilbur has never been more passionate.

During the final quarter of the 20th century, immigrants from non-European nations started to arrive in greater numbers than ever before. Frequently, these new Canadians came from non-Judeo-Christian backgrounds. These poets, who have become our poets, eventually began to publish books and find a growing readership. Canadian literature was no longer based on the old British and European models. It rapidly became cosmopolitan. And more recently still, Indigenous voices have begun to be heard. It must be noted that our two most significant singer-songwriters are Buffy Sainte-Marie (a Cree born on Saskatchewan's Piapot First Nation) and Robbie Robertson (a Mohawk from the Six Nations First Nation in Ontario). A People's Poet at heart, Sainte-Marie has recently said, "The job of a poet is to get information across in a way that's effective in making change."[1]

While the process of broadening Canadian culture beyond its Judeo-Christian/European roots has certainly not been without controversy, multiculturalism, a "dirty word" in some quarters, is the reality of 21st century Canada. One result of these developments is that Canadian literature has emerged as a world literature in the full sense of the term. It is my view, and the message of this anthology, that the poetry being written today in Canada is as important, and as varied, as any other English-language poetry. Our present poetry is as fine as it was in prior generations, and it is more diverse due to the recent injection of non-European influences. Canada has truly evolved into a "united nations" of poetry. Should we welcome these new immigrants and their contributions to our literature? As the good Dr. Acorn wrote: "A Canadian by choice, the truest kind."[2] In this respect, Canadian poetry has never been stronger.

James Deahl
Sarnia, 2018

1. *Reader's Digest* Volume 191, Number 1,144 (November 2017). Page 38. Print.
2. Inscribed by Milton Acorn in the editor's copy of *I've Tasted My Blood*.

Robert S. Acorn

Bedspread

She cannot forgive
the washing of her soul
the caustic soap
the cold rinse water
the relentless pressure
of the wringer
and being hung to dry
on a steel clothesline
held in place with
old-fashioned stick pins
then lifted to the wind
by a Mi'kmaq clothesline pole
without real hope.

She nourishes her hurt
and holds to shame
like soot spots and the green
bowman Robin Hood
on pillowslips and sheets
which fade from view
after successive washings.

She asked to be saved
but didn't envision
being cast as a plaything
with no citizenship
for appeal to Caesar.

Yet disillusionment
keeps dissipating
like trying to remember pain
with a baby in her arms
the clean clothes
smelling sweet
after being outside
blown dry in the wind.

Passchendaele

One after the other a Canadian
Black Watch detail left the catwalk
over the mud on the run
each holding his Lee-Enfield
barrel higher than the butt
moving to the rhythm
of his stride.

Straight-brim steel helmets and
forty-pound packs felt weightless
as a German machine gun
rattled steel jacketed bullets
overtop spraying mud off
the rim of the moat-like
series of shell holes.

The reconnaissance patrol
had to get across the muddy
and blood-curdled water at the bottom
of the explosion dug trench.

The corporal didn't hesitate
to jump, though he might drown
in the bog, but luckily his left foot
struck something submerged.

All ten men placed a
foot in the exact spot
while jumping safely across.

As the last man landed on
the human stepping stone
an arm wearing a German tunic
surfaced waving them God's speed.

The passions of the recently
dead were with the living
things looking differently
under the surface.

Sylvia Adams

No Pictures of Him Smiling

> *Tones sound and roar and storm about me until*
> *I have set them down in notes.*
> – Ludwig van Beethoven

Once, when I stood on my father's stool
to reach the keyboard, he shouted like thunder
till I thought I'd go deaf.
The rhythm of his beatings echoes yet.

Luck is a clash of symbols splitting the air.
Tantalizing, mercurial, gone in a quarter-note.
Imagine sitting at Mozart's feet
piano keys trembling with joy's delirium
just as a messenger summons me back to Bonn,
my mother dying, my father awash in drink.

Orphaned, my brothers followed me to Vienna.
My life became the cadence of combing knots
from their hair, sending them out with baskets.
Music rumbled like thunder in my brain,
burned my belly — endless strains of frustration
till I was deaf to my brothers' idle chatter
and the *sturm und drang* of their women.

If I wash myself in the morning,
a bucket over my head, that is all
the time I have for parochial niceties;
every syllable, every note shudders,
icy fingers incinerating crescendos.

So what if the ladies snicker behind their fans —
dutifully, to please their men —
I know they love me, but husbands and fathers
insist they taunt me, ugly boor half-crazy.
And the nephew I fought to raise:
philistine as the lyrics bawled by applewomen.
Keyboard, washboard, all the same to him,
racing me to the grave.

I've always been in love but you know that.
You've read my letters, sent and unsent, mused
over my Beloved, sighed at impossibilities. But
let me have my secrets. The *music* is for you.
I plough flutes to their deepest earthtones, lift
trombones cloudwards, sweep the sky symphonic.

Princes and vegetable farmers are all the same to me.
The nobly born rise legion, births trumpeting titles:
pigs who grunt and squeal through my sonatas.
Whose duty is it to bow? *There is only one of me.*

Fitting that I should die at the peak of the storm.
You can hear it yet.

Becky D. Alexander

Buried Deep
    details from a memoir by Sergeant Jim Alexander (MM)
    Lincoln and Welland Regiment, Holland, 1945

In the kitchen, from the doorway to the hearth,
lying on the floor like some colossal cigarette —
a log, one end in the fire, burning slowly
as flames surround a bubbling pot.

It mystified the Canadian soldiers, those kept
after the war — troops retained
to rebuild a battered country, one
that refused to be swallowed back into the sea.

The explanation provided to the curious,
Because the Nazis took all of our metal:
axes, pitchforks, scythes and hoes, even kitchen knives —
a last ditch effort to build more weapons.

Allied saviours shared meals of boiled tulip bulbs:
'the most gawd-awful things you ever ate'
along with Red Cross chocolate and rationed tins
of bully beef: bitter meals of freedom.

Under our barn, wrapped in oiled burlap,
we have our tractor and plow — buried bits cloistered away
following the final swoop of the flag of black on red.
They never found them. Soon, we will plant.

Donna Allard

map

she is a map, border-less,
with aged skin-scape, alive
and yet dying

down familiar roads that detour
to unfamiliar shores

under summer sun'watch
she dry heaves pebbles, stars
and unknowns

a strangers glance beckons,
falls between the cracks,
the moment : a still photo

haunting
. . . isn't it
being route-less

Rosemary Aubert

Made In China

At the museum we see
a boat that set sail from China
for Europe
a thousand years ago.

We gasp at the treasures
at the very idea
that something so old
lies before us
as fresh as the day
that everyone on it
died.

As we round the corner
we see an exhibit
of the cargo
preserved in a cold and waveless sea.

There are among the treasures
five hundred clay bowls.
They are perfectly round
glazed
bearing floral designs
that we recognize as Chinese.

Because it is the same shape
the same impervious shine
the same flowers
as on the ones we bought
yesterday at the dollar store.

The museum is full
of timeless treasures
but none as precious as these
which hold a thousand years
up to our lips
for a sip of tea.

The Plague 1665 - 1666

Men who would be spared, fled
until the empty streets were filled with wolves
who finding nothing left to eat
sank back into the fetid wood
and ate the ones who hid there.

Men who stayed in town perished too.
No quarantine secure enough.
No lock sufficient.
No lie.
No pretence.
No escape
from the warden, the wagon, the pit.

I could write of the agony:
the dagger in the skull
the devil's dark kisses: buboes and rash.
Breath sealed forever in the lungs.

The doors of Cambridge slammed me out.
I went to an old pure place
and there among the fields, I staked my claim.
So write instead of my haven
Among the clean and cleansing stars.

Henry Beissel

4 from: **Stones to Harvest**

(fall)

After the pizzicato rains
last night my shadow leans
across wet matted leaves
tall against the glistening
black trunks of maples
stretching naked into dawn.

    I listen to the cool
    blues in the sky.
    You're the woods
    and the wind whistling
    a sullen air
    for a solitary dance.

Soon the frost
will rob the birds
of their song
leaving us
to our loving.

    You're the melancholy
    beneath the bark of trees
    mellowing into winter.

    *

(winter)

Stamping its feet on the roof
and howling down the chimney
a furious east wind pulls the clouds
down from the sky, rips them apart
and blows the pieces into a white
frenzy of whirling dances and drifts
till heaven and earth are one
vast vortex of spinning crystals.

    The pine-trees heave their branches
    like wings, struggling to take flight
    and threatening, once airborne
    to swoop down and drive away
    winter's wild and murderous hordes.

Blizzards pack every niche and crevice
and stop at nothing short of walls.

    Whatever feels or breathes
    must find shelter now
    from their ice-cold fury:

        Our bodies are not
          fortress enough
        though we plug
        every crack
        with a passion.

    *   >>>

(spring)

The young sun raises flowers
from dead leaves and greens
the fallow fields panting
with moist aromatic breath.

    A tractor stutters down the pasture.
    Steel hands rip the earth, bringing
    worms to light and stones to harvest.

Birds breed camouflaged
but the black-faced cardinal,
too early for rose or poppy,
puts a touch of blood
in the half-naked trees.

    The wind bends shadows
    and blows your hair
    into torrents of desire.

Our moments of happiness
are in the hands of clocks
with nerves of steel.

    *

(summer)

The force that pulls
trees and grasses
through the eye of light
vertically up to the sky
pushes their roots
through silt and stone
down to the dark
pole of all beginnings.

    At noon every flower
    sings hosanna to the sun
    over a ground bass figure
    in a major key.

Green green green
are wind and odour
and greener still
the drone of bugs.

    You dance through my heart
    like a fantasy
    for violin and piano.

Manifesto in Times of War

Tell the enemy this:
that missiles can no more blow up the human spirit
than tanks can crush an idea.
Guns are the weapons of the impotent,
and I wouldn't trade one line of true poetry
for a thousand of them. The blood flowers
in a poem while bombs can only spill it.
Shrapnel can shatter glass and shred the flesh
but it cannot silence the song in a people's heart.

Tell the enemy this:
that our missiles fly on imagination's wings —
they're poems aimed to explode in the heart
with all the violence of love and compassion.
It may flatter princes to think the sword mightier
than the pen, but we have the last word.
The true poet pioneers paths of freedom
and places on the future's mouth a brotherhood kiss
with the rage of a rainstorm that makes the desert bloom.

Tell the enemy this:
that every man, woman and child wears a helmet
poets hammer from a metal harder than any steel —
the metal of their faith in creation.
You can tear a person limb from limb
but you cannot sever a song from the listening heart,
and when your missiles long rust in scrapyards
today's tears will have watered the desert
to make yesterday's laughter blossom into tomorrow's love.

Tell the enemy this: Yes,
we are still writing poems, and if your grenades
blow off our hands, we'll sing them into the future.

Amaryllis

Sirens scream at the drowsy city
as an ambulance chases a silent stalker
that lies in ambush in the dark passageways
connecting the body's many dwellings
to the extremities of the heart.

A victim choking in the killer's hold
is snatched from certain death at zero hour
and delivered to emergency. The attack
is registered, compressed into dates and data,
the patient poked, probed and injected.

The stalker refuses to surrender
his vital statistics, but medication
puts him in his place, and his intended victim
takes heart as he is wheeled to a ward
for the surgeon's inquest and sentence.

The long dark tunnel from emergency
is chilly and foreboding. Fear creeps
into the mind's folds. The heart, worn
from the burdens of living, falters:
will it rally to beat the odds in the morning?

Tracks crisscross the ceiling of each ward
to run curtains round the solitude
of those in pain. Little of what is left
of their pride huddles in hives of hope
where tiny flames strobe-light the will to live.

Patients pushed and pulled in wheelchairs
or on hospital gurneys between labs, surgery
and their cubicles, mostly men, mostly old,
semi-private, semi-conscious, semi-alive
and semi-dead, their manhood diminished

till even their patience goes limp. And I
grow weary of waiting among the promises
of well-meaning doctors and the solicitations
of smiling nurses. I know the killer bides his time
in the blood and the heart cannot be institutionalized.

Dawn presses a grey blanket damp against the window.
I hear the winter wind whistle a dirge in the streets below,
blowing flurries of snow horizontally across the cold light.
Five storeys above the just awakening Ottawa traffic
I feel my years like a heavy weight in my flesh and bones.

And there, at the centre of my anxiety,
between drab hospital walls and insipid meals,
an explosion of blood-red petals — an amaryllis!
Nine blossoms succulent as passion, a gift of love
feeding the flames in one of my nine lives.

Buds rose on sturdy green legs hour by hour
from the first day of my confinement
unfolded till they towered above the ailing
wannabe living forever and a day —
a cluster of floral flesh and blood

like a circle of dancers suspended in mid-air,
mouths wide open, all lips and loving,
anthers tonguing the clinical air,
their crimson petals velvet skirts flaring —
a tableau to trump mortality for another day.

The sirens were silent when I went home,
the blood once more coursing freely
through the re-enforced tunnels in the flesh,
an amaryllis singing a Renaissance glee
to the tune of a newly enchanted heart.

Henge

They raised the stones with music and star fire
Orchestrated in the bright moonlight
Of the longest day.

Hundreds of ranks of trained bards
And mages in their own right
Ranged around the plain
One rank for each set of uprights and lintel

One master to lead
And direct their shimmering energies
One master to control the power
That sets the lintel gently atop the uprights

The power of their music hangs brilliant
In the moonlit air
Shimmering and coalescing over the plain
The granite stones pulse warmly and glow
As they move and dance into place

It is done
The master turns and bows
To welcome the Sun
This morning of the longest day

The ranks of bards bow
And raise shining eyes
As the Sun bathes them
In the first flush of dawn light

The master smiles
The stones settle into their beds
The Sun's rays shine true
Locking the stones in place

The song rises with the Sun
Blooming from the bards
From the granite stone itself
The God and Goddess dance
Across the lintel stones

Sharon Berg

Prophesy
      for Al Purdy

I was twelve
when I dreamed of you,
my older brother's father,
a man who made his living
from words and innuendo.

I dreamed my brother and I
were at a mall, made arrangements
to meet back at the central pool.
In this dream, the pool held a tree,
bark stripped, branches naked.

When brother and I met again,
you stopped by with another child
close to my brother's age,
explaining nothing to either one
though both boys were your sons.

There was frivolity in your greeting,
no truth in our interactions,
and soon I wanted to be away
from this place of myth
and denial.

When I met you as a grown up,
in real life, you were just like that,
sweeping in with your bravado,
not thinking about consequences,
tearing other lives apart.

>>>

You have passed over now,
even your method of leaving straining
the people you have left behind.
So just now, I understand that dream
when I was twelve as a prophesy.

That tree in the pool was naked and dead,
no branches sprouting leaves,
just as your sons had no children,
your branch of the family
leaving the gene pool.

June Sunset-Alberta - *Nancy Bell*

Steven Michael Berzensky *(Mick Burrs)*

Breathing In the Bees
    for Andrew Suknaski

"Listen to us," their wings whisper. "We insist.
We've some sacred images for you."

I'm the poet. They're the uninvited guests,
the spirits of the forgotten and the dead.

They hover above the boxes of books on the floor
and the yellow news clippings cluttering my desk.

They tap on my skull relentlessly, these bees!
They weave through the leaves of my hair.

Soon, some of these intruders sway
on the stalks of my fingers.

What choice do I have?
They won't let me rest.

Once more I permit them to rebuild with words
the honeycombed chambers of my heart.

Notes on Mandelstam

1.

Anything can be poured into a poem
      as long as it smells of life
        or reeks of death or stares down
like the cold half moon

2.

Pack all you know into the fewest lines
        the only baggage you're allowed
      to take with you
into exile, into darkness

3.

truth
is dangerous
    poems
    are dangerous
        you can
          die for poetry

        Heart

      it is always becoming a poem
      this furnace, this fire
      in a corner of the body's dark

      this is the place that burns
      whatever has been broken

Clara Blackwood

Persephone Unbound

> *A Persephone woman is susceptible to depression when she is dominated and limited by people who keep her bound to them.*
> – Jean Shinoda Bolen, Goddesses in Everywoman

At some point, she breaks entirely.
Does not yet know
this is the beginning of her freedom.
The weight of sadness, an iron crypt
immovable whose structure finally
collapses under its own strain.
Complicated further by unsolicited guests.

Most days she considers herself
a natural sadomasochist —
as the sun to the moon,
bird to the branch,
Jupiter to Europa —
no cycling past it.

But this time she will flee those
who try to bind her,
develop an allergic reaction —
a rash on the skin,
her upper back turning bright red
from inner heat and repressed rage
underneath a heavy Canadian winter coat.

Robert A. Boates

Late September
for Brian

Driving north to Athabasca
through seasons fighting
for conquest of an afternoon.
A crack across the windshield
suggests lightning; a bolt sealed
in a paperweight like a scorpion,
its tail poised to strike.

The day is full of slaughter.
Sleet-covered cattle wait to be led
to market. Deer evade searching eyes.
Smaller animals remain concealed, for death
wears wings and is always swift.

We are small beneath this sky,
travelling toward the horizon.
That rainbow in the distance,
a sickle, a promise.

The Good Life

It's an alarm that doesn't go off.
A rush for the toilet.
A broken dresser drawer.
Torn stockings. A radio
station that won't stay tuned.
A lunch left behind. It's an
outdated circuit breaker.
A fire hazard; rent day.
It's Mr. Dressup and The Friendly Giant.
It's dirty laundry on bedroom floors
and writing while cleaning the house.
It's a four-year-old with leukemia.
Hospital visits. A multitude of needles.
It's a working wife and mother.
A fridge full of beer. Milk rings
and Rice Krispies on the table.
Affidavits in the mail;
a crazy ex-husband.
Dogs in the garbage. Rats
in the produce at I.G.A.

It's an empty can of Comet.
Baptists at the door.
It's children playing in the street;
skinned knees and elbows.
It's wilted birthday roses.
It's ants in the pantry.
Kraft Dinner again.
It's the Victorian Order of Nurses.
It's a broken vacuum cleaner.
Hugs and kisses at bedtime.
Endless pots of tea. Smoking
on the back porch. The moon
smiling mauve. Bats
against a purple sky.
It's conversation in the bath.
Making love every night.
It's never getting enough sleep
and not caring. It's routine.
It's monotony and monogamy.
It's company: it's never
looking back.

Kent Bowman

Vacancy at the Blues Barbershop (Chicago)

What a lonely place behind this closed barbershop door
as if the hour glass had run out of sand,
but the vacancy sign remained
as a sad reminder of a bygone time.
Did this barber become so depressed by the blues
that he packed up his razor and scissors
and left in search of anything resembling joy.
Or was he so infused with sadness that he died by his own hand —
slain by a blues riff played by Chicago's most desolate guitar player.

Let us pay homage to this long suffering cutter
who heard one blues song too often and took his own life
rather than listen to a final grim chorus by this relentless note slayer.
I can see the obituary now:
Faithful barber slain by the blues —
One more good man cut down
to cut no more.

Frances Boyle

Pelican Narrows

I make myself look away from my daughter, sealed
into an envelope of blankets, quiet now but too white.
Fighting down panic, I attend to details:
watch the pilot steer, raising and lowering the wheel
as he turns it; feel the plane bank wide. The rumble
never lessens. That short distance on the map — Jan Lake
to Pelican Narrows — is now an endless smudge
of forest laced with water.

Then a scrubby stretch of runway stands out, light
against the dark trees. Shirtsleeve weather back home,
here I shiver on the early evening tarmac,
fleeces and three-season bags left at the campsite with our friends.
Attendants jog from the quonset to the plane, abandoning
artifacts I make out in its window's yellow light:
a teapot and thick mugs on an oilcloth-covered table,
a sugar bowl with its lid off. Another pilot signs for my child,
acknowledges receipt of this pale package they unload,
gently reload on a bigger plane.

My daughter is taller than me, a better paddler by far.
Oh, but how could I bring a girl into the wild
to be bit by a rusted relic of a trap? I'd cauterize that gash
with tears if I could, propose any bargain —
my own leg? both arms? The pelican (in her piety
they used to say) would nourish her young with her own blood.
What mother wouldn't, I ask as the plane starts to climb
eastward towards Flin Flon.

Mary Lee Bragg

My Mother's Birds

*I snipped the tail feathers
off my grandmother's canary.*

My mother's memory reaches
across the century, to the year
of the Spanish flu,
a small child sent away to a safer place.
She finds the flower room, quilt blocks,
sewing scissors too close to the cage
and tail feathers between the bars.

*That darn bird didn't sing
until they grew back, and
Grandma was mad at me
the whole time.*

I remember other birds,
ducks piled iridescent
and smooth on our porch,
cold and soft-necked,
passive to pet.

My mother plucked the feathers,
snowstorms of down around her feet.
She drew their guts into a pail —
corrugated blue gizzards, purple livers,
intestines like earthworms —
her hand red to the elbow.

We ate roast duck and spat
buckshot onto our plates.

And above her graveside
geese vee toward the Chinook arch.
My brother says *Honk if you like Rachel.*

And they do,
    they do.

Allan Briesmaster

To Du Fu, after 13 Centuries
   712 -770. *He had no idea he would
   become one of China's most-loved poets.*

Such disparate worlds. But you call
far-across the abysses. From frail
hut after hut of right words, begun
in a once grand society bled
by insane ceaseless wars: worn down,
bowed as you were in ill health,
withdrawn beside the long waters
under desolate cirrus, wan moon
that, even so, gave, like an ablution,
your constellated lines: their fluent
image of being.
             Poor and obscured,
seldom back home or for long at each refuge,
in threadbare cold, in sadness,
the fleeting reprieve with a friend,
the helpless compassion, bald grief, your cry
still issues its power to pierce
the dust laid down over ages
of collapsing kingdoms' ruins,
perennial guises of greed, wrath and pride,
the murk also of the clumsy translations —

to glass and distil and bring near
the most remote visions for those
who sip your moonlit wine as they rock
slowly there in the thin
but miraculous boat of the brain
that slips past blithe or brutish denial
and scorn of the historic warnings,
decline of mere solidarity
in a thoughtful existence. Of care. You,
who breathe improbable brotherhood
past every mask of despair.

In Flight

How thin the wings that lift us to our air
over the fleeting ground — that stiffly bear
the shakes of turbulence. Titanium,
bolted and cut into severest lightness,
at proven angles mastering such height.

Along our own plane, where we serve as pilot,
nobody mapped the final landing spot.

One solo charter. Hardly comprehending
our ported views, the clouds that streak their layer
to the horizon. Seeing how all we eye,
so large yet finite, races out of light.

And now we feel consumption's gauges quaver,
fuel and power drain, while wings fatigue.

What does it ever leave, beyond the contrail —
that speck, blinking against the gorge of night?

Ronnie R. Brown

For Keeps
> *Thoughts on the 50th anniversary of
> the D-Day invasion, June 6th, 1994.*

The television cameras love them,
track a mottled, vein-corded hand
as it traces the letters
of a fallen comrade's name; zoom
in on a tear as it slides
down a craggy face.

Fifty years ago, the voice-over reminds,
many of these "old soldiers"
were still in their teens.

Moved by patriotism, wanderlust,
or the dream of new boots, three squares
every day and money, too,
they lied about their age, signed
on the line. Children,
some no more than thirteen,
donning uniforms, marching away.

Upstairs, days from turning seventeen,
my own son sits, eyes focused
on the computer's screen. If I listen
I can hear the muted sounds
of explosions, guns, as, joy stick in hand,
he struggles to save some fantasy world
from simulated catastrophe.

I try to convince myself he is safe,
will never wear a uniform, march off,
gun in hand, to defend democracy,
will not come home years later,
changed as his grandfather did,
will never know the nightmares
that rend a soldier's sleep; try to forget,
if only for a moment, that a click
away, television cameras are focused
on other mothers' children. Live
via satellite they stand, winning smiles
on their adolescent faces,
holding guns
that should be toys,
acting all grown up,
playing for keeps.

Thoughts After The Carnage

Over the shouts of NRA enthusiasts demanding
their rights, a father speaks about his dead
son, their last goodbye, his promise they'd
finish that gingerbread house "tonight."

One of the surviving children can't bear
the sound of the doorbell. He'd watched
as his classmates went down like targets
in a carnival game; is well-schooled in
"taking turns;" knows he's next.

In schools everywhere teachers ask kids
"Who knows their numbers?" Watch
as hands shoot up, hear the rat-a-tat
of children chanting: onetwothree . . . in
Newtown that day, the counting stopped dead.

Think of a suburban woman and her assault
weapons. Imagine her taking her troubled
son to the gun range; teaching him to shoot.
Think carefully, then list everything
that's wrong with this picture.

After the massacre, thousands send toys
and flowers. After the massacre tens
of thousands join the NRA. "Change
will come," a spokesperson on TV
assures, "But incrementally — one
catastrophe at a time."

Imagine waiting outside your child's school,
Imagine listening to an announcement
telling you: "If your child is not with you
he or she is probably a fatality."
One hundred and fifty four bullet casings
are found. Try not to think about the way
automatic gunfire eats through flesh.

Try not to think about six year old
bodies torn apart.

"Are they with the angels now?"
a surviving child asks. Tell me,
how should we reply?

An Object Believed to be Human Remains

Here, over here, can't you see me?

A few short weeks ago we walked hand
in hand in this park, my lover
and I. Now my hands, my feet
are evidence. Now my family
must face the horror, the disgrace
I have brought down on them. I wanted
excitement. Relished the freedom
this new country brought. Sought
out this lover, craved all he was: rock
star handsome, exotic, wild and oh
so dangerous.

Those who glimpse me, my face
dug into the earth, doubt their eyes. Assume:
stone, plastic toy, or maybe an animal skull. My jaws
agape in a last scream, offer
insects easy entry. Those industrious
creatures, along with the passage of time, the hot,
humid days, have led to my putrefaction, have made
unidentifiable to topography of my once pleasant
but ordinary face.

"Over here!" a voice cries out
and, at last, I am found, lifted
taken away. Soon, reunion. My
mother will have a son to bury. My story
will become a cautionary tale. Name
forgotten, I will live on only as an object
lesson: that of the dismembered man.
Though somewhere, somehow, I pray
a trace of that which made me
all too human
remains.

NOTE: *In June, 2012, Luka Magnotta murdered and dismembered his lover, Lin Jun, mailing his hands and feet to four locations (including two political party headquarters). Lin Jun's head was discovered a month later in Montreal's Angrignon Park.*

April Bulmer

Buffalograss Jail

Native men in a cage
pace like clipped birds.
Their brown hands
grasp the bars,
imagining bark.

Medicines in a little bag
around their thick necks:
crushed herbs and sage.
The gentle scent of healing.

I wonder what they dream:
rain in the bush:
the way a lake will open
like a woman,
shiver in the heat.

I bring them braids of sweet grass.
Then photos of Fox, Bear, Muskrat and Deer.
My men are now broken and free —
haunted and hunted like me.

Skins

In the morning,
even the Sun kneels
in His pew.
I fall to my knees too
and the fabric
of my old soul
tears and bleeds.
Remember a feather
in the dirt
a snake skin by the river.

And in dreams
I crawl from my body:
its hair and its bones.
Carcass pocked by the touch
of men and weather.

Rebecca Clifford

Turkey Vultures

I stroll out to check the beans,
        make sure fungus, weevils
are few   far   between

Air is heavy   humid
I am   sweat slicked   irritable

A shadow grazes my shoulder
        another follows suit
                daring closer
        dusting pollened gusts against my back,
a fire wind

                I've stood inert too long

They scribe languid thermal circles
        through steam saturated air

I stir, stride barnward,
        defiance in my throat
                "I'm not dead yet!"

Patrick Connors

Exit Poll
    Advice to the New Leader

1. Promises are made to be broken,
               — like rotten eggs —
  but not until the morning
                  after the election.

2. The current state of affairs
     is merely your reaction
  to mistakes *others* made in the past.

3. Give the people what they want
    — visions of fresh young faces,
    sunny summer picnics, and
    reduced deficit spending —
  but don't let them realize
    a better tomorrow.

4. Because the next administration
                will have to
     take it
  back!

5. Fiscal restraint is what makes
       our civilization *great* —
  or, at least, it will keep
       the current system
  chugging along a bit longer.

6. A balanced budget
         should *almost* make up
            for all those pesky poor people.

Tony Cosier

Saw Music

A sound that even in memory
puts you square in a place.
Cambridge, let's say, or Keswick.
You see the exact street, every alcove,
every brick in a wall
and always in the rain it seems
or on the edge of rain.

Shrill notes quavered eerily
though saw and player viewed close
were natural enough you could see the sound.
In the wobbled flash and flicker of the sheet lightning blade.
In the back and forth caress of the bow crossing teeth.
In the curved wood handle at the base
and the man wrapped round.

He was invariably alone and ever a composite,
himself and the one who taught him
and the one before that
until you had them all there
and everything else . . .
every nail in the railway tie
every ping of a pebble on tin
sand glint, turf grit, wet quarry stone.

And never once did he stop.
It was always you that left
maybe dropping a coin in a hat to a nod
as you moved on out through street and crowd
still stirred, still listening backward
absorbing whatever tiny scrap you could
of the diminished wavering cry.

Stone Steps

They start from the base of the steps, squatting to squint
Along the drainage line, wincing at ruts, taking note
Of silt in lumps fanned from black cracked joints.
They lift slates, extract blocks from grit
And lay out a runic algebra over the lawn.
With tractor and shovel, they dig the whole gap out
Beyond the retaining wall. And fill it again,
Not the way it was, but with stones in a net
Crushed to shuck water and keep shape.
Across the rumble of the rolling drum,
Over the trowel's scrape and slubbering slap,
They speak of tradition, weather, things to come,
Root one another into the here and now.
They set in reverse blocks beneath steps with care
And finish in the only way they know,
Scouring the site. They leave nothing to show they were there
But a trim ascending welcomer granite-tough
And tightly chiseled sharp as the face of a cliff.

Lorna Crozier

The Mask

She kept the mask, not knowing
what to do with it. That hard plastic skin
molded to the shape of his face, fitted over
his head and attached to the treatment table.
It sits in a coffee-maker box
on the closet shelf above the shoes
she's kept as well, though all the clothes
are gone. She tells no one. It's been three years —
her friends and son wouldn't understand.

Tonight she drops his shoes in a garbage bag,
relaxes her gaze, something she's learned
to do in yoga so she doesn't really see.
Then she takes down the box that promises
Maximum Capacity, Brew Strength Control,
Easy-to-Fill Water Reservoir.

She opens the lid: there it is, his face —
an empty husk, cut-outs for the mouth and nose,
none for the eyes. When asked if he wanted them,
he'd said no. She thought he'd made that choice
so he wouldn't see the blank expression
of the radiographer, the cold machine
that promised nothing. Later she wondered if,
in some strange way, he was getting ready.
Not only lying still but blind now, too,
the table sliding him headfirst into a fire.

He'd practiced death so well,
when she brought him home, she kept checking
with a feather pulled from a pillow.
In the choir, he'd learned to turn a single breath
into so much sound it filled their church.
It undermined the light.

More than any photograph taken near the last,
the cast holds his likeness. She runs her fingers over
his nose, the shells of his ears, his jaw's parentheses.
What disturbs her most is the mouth, the hope-
lessness of the opening his lips surround.

She lies down on what she calls *their* bed
and dons the mask. It doesn't fit, of course,
her face is small inside it. Three years.
She trembles under the duvet that must be
stuffed with snow. Her eyes won't open.
She doesn't know how to end what she's begun.

Time Studies

The watches in the Good Will Store are the watches
of the dead. If you put one to your ear, you'll hear
the sound of snow falling.

    *

You wonder why so many old women collect small spoons.
You don't, though you are old now too. Everything you stir,
everything you spoon into your mouth demands something bigger.
As if your tongue was an implant from a giant, as if your gut
demanded a wheelbarrow of meatloaf, a cloud fat with hail
the size of baseballs, the size of a common, ordinary grief.

    *

God draws a life. Then begins to rub it out
with the eraser on his pencil. It always smears but does
its job. God, used to saving, is saving paper. He sharpens
the pencil, licks the lead and starts again.
This is, you dare to say, his *flawed* concept of time.
When his mouth is dry, he draws nothing. Well then:
the blankness of the page lasts for what seems forever
if you're mortal, if you're thirsty, if you live on earth.

    *

There are three kinds of adverbs: adverbs of manner,
of place, of time. In that order: *slowly, here, now.*
Little gods of grammar, adverbs are what you pray to.
They answer no one — indifferently, variously, mysteriously,
enigmatically, never. Their dogma demands you place *only*
only where it belongs.

    *

In the world of the Good Will Store, good will is not for sale
though for some reason there are lots of men's pajama bottoms,
hardly worn. Tea cups. Small spoons, too.
Once there was a big tomato with a stem to grip and the top
came off. It was a cookie jar, stale crumbs and chocolate chips

littered the bottom. Its lesson: you never know
what's in the hollow inside anything, especially a cane
carried by a foreign, old-time spy, especially the human heart.

    *

Tomorrow and tomorrow and tomorrow . . .
The antimony, the petty pace, no physicist can say it better:
Poets are the true scientists of time.
The *never, never, never, never, never*
Lear wailed when Cordelia died.

My Last Erotic Poem

Who wants to hear about
two old farts getting it on
in the back seat of a Buick,
in the garden shed among vermiculite,
in the kitchen where we should be drinking
ovaltine and saying no? Who wants to hear
about 26 years of screwing,
our once-not-unattractive flesh
now loose as unbaked pizza dough
hanging between two hands before it's tossed?

Who wants to hear about two old lovers
slapping together like water hitting mud,
hair where there shouldn't be
and little where there should,
my bunioned foot sliding
up your bony calf, your calloused hands
sinking in the quickslide of my belly,
our faithless bums crepitous, collapsed?

We have to wear our glasses to see down there!

    >>>

When you whisper what you want I can't hear,
but do it anyway, and somehow get it right. Face it,
some nights we'd rather eat a Haagen Dazs ice cream bar
or watch a movie starring Nick Nolte who looks worse than us.
Some nights we'd rather stroke the cats.

Who wants to know when we get it going
we're revved up, like the first time — honest —
like the first time, if only we could remember it,
our old bodies doing what you know
bodies do, worn and beautiful and shameless.

The Underworld

I.
The River Styx has no beginning,
no end. You can't row its waters,
it's just a metaphor for grief.
But the dog is real. People like to tell you
their dog is a Rescue Dog.
This one isn't.
He's set his coat on fire.

II.
Mother, mother, you say, hoping she'll appear.
You didn't know she had that in her —
so much anguish. So many damaged wings.

III.
The poet said all wounds close at night.
They don't. There is the bird torn open.
There is the naked heart. The gash in the fir tree.
Perhaps it is morning here. Wait a few hours.
The sutures may happen. A bone-needle
threaded with an eternal sleeper's drool.

IV.
Not as dark as you thought.
Something gives off a kind of light.
What makes you inconsolable is the silence.
No wind in leaves. No grass speaking.
The shadows are more than shadows.
And there is a lot of waiting.
Only one doctor and all these cities of the dead.

Phillip Crymble

Nursery

      An early summer afternoon in Glasgow, and we've come
to see exotic flora in the West End's glazed conservatories.

      Lost in careless conversation with your sister, you wander
off to look at tree ferns, palms and succulents — leave me

      fiddling with the two pence piece I found on Byres Road.
The Kibble Palace koi pond's like a magnet for young

      families — children point, ask questions, and I feel at once
how lovely and how lonesome life can be. Out in the gardens

      there's a limousine — the Scottish bride concealed by tinted
windows. Two men in rented morning coats — the fathers,

      almost certainly — seem purposeful, agreed. Between
my finger and my thumb I roll the coin. When you come

      back to me it's yours. Some things aren't meant to keep.
Wish carefully, then drop it in the water. Watch it sink.

Robert Currie

Thief

I barely had it stuffed in my pocket
when the hand seized my shoulder.
A clerk dragged me to the back of the store,
up half a dozen stairs to the manager's office.
"This boy's a thief," was what she said
when she let me go, my shoulder burning.

"Hand it over," said the manager. "Right now."
He sat at his desk on a wooden chair with wheels,
and he spun toward me, his voice
a rusty spade slicing through gravel.
I dug into my pocket and hauled it out,
my hand shaking, a Roy Rogers cap gun.
"Now, let's have your name and phone number."

I might have lied, but I stammered the truth.
"Come on!" he said. "Speak up so I can hear you."
I could still make up a name, give him the number
of my friend whose parents were never home,
but no, not me, I told the truth a second time.
He whirled back to his desk and dialled.
Oh Lord, my father, he was talking to my father.
When he finished, he wheeled toward me.
"That's that," he said. "You leave this store
and don't come back. Your old man will deal with you."

I got out of there fast, but beyond the outside door
my feet would hardly move, my father waiting at home.
It was already suppertime when I reached the subway
beneath the tracks, but I leaned on the guard rail,
counting every boxcar that rattled overhead.
When finally I dragged myself up the hill and home,
I stood in the backyard, not once glancing at the door
where my father would be waiting. Would he spank me?
I hoped he would. Somehow I knew already,
that when at last I raised my eyes to his,
I'd never forget the look on his face.

Because I Never

Because I never learned to dance
I stood fixed in the high school gym,
music blasting around me while I gazed
at the backboard, the hoop, its net
dropping a mesh of shadows on the floor.
I told the guys I could hardly wait
for tomorrow's basketball practice
when what I craved was nerve enough
to walk the empty space in front of me
— like a soldier, upright and brave, reckless,
no doubt, slowly traversing no-man's land —
stepping away from this group of guys
toward that distant line of girls
who laughed and talked so easily together
as if they never noticed when a guy
found a way to cross that vacant floor.
I tried not to stare at the grade eleven girl
who stood fifth from the end of the line, silver
ear rings flashing, pony tail bobbing on her shoulder.
I stayed within the shadows of the net
as if held there by a giant spider's web.

Because I never learned to dance
my mother spoke to Mrs. Loveridge
and hired her daughter, Lucrezia,
to teach me how to jive, and for five weeks
every Wednesday after school I descended
to their basement rumpus room, praying
no friend of mine had seen me sneak inside,
and there I tried to beat my feet to the rhythms
of Bill Haley and the Comets, Lucrezia at ease
and liquid in my arms, stepping perfectly, whirling
when I threw her out with one hand, caught her
with the other, spinning her behind my back,
twirling her beneath my arm, me already fearing
what I knew was bound to be the truth,
I'd never learn to dance
with any other girl.

David Day

Just Say 'No' to Family Values
*With apologies to Allen Ginsberg, Charles Manson,
Nancy Reagan and Martin Luther King.*

I've seen the best minds of my generation
Destroyed by accountancy.
I've seen blue-eyed and golden-haired youth poisoned
And driven to utter insanity by an overdose of wedlock.

I've seen young wild-haired prophets
And new-age goddesses
Twisted and disfigured by mortgage rates,
By bank loans, by car payments,
By credit cards bills, by exorbitant parking fees.

I've seen inspired genius
And virginal innocence sacrificed
On the altar of the Goddess of the P.T.A. Bake Counters,
And on the green swards of the diabolical
Throbbing Lawnmower God
With his demonic tabernacle choir
Of plastic pink flamingos.

I've seen the divine philosophies
And utterances of young Platos
Mistaken for the mindless yapping
Of Mickey Mouse's Dog.

I've seen satellite television short circuit
The minds of artists
And cause their eyeballs to implode and melt down
When confronted by the tasteless pastel saccharine terrorism
Of 'Care Bears' and 'My Little Ponies'

I've seen enchanted poets
Offer up their god-given golden tongues
As small tokens of sacrifice

For a steady job in advertising,
A triple-A rated secure medical and dental plan,
A paid-up fund for the kid's college fees,
A new spin dryer,
And a stupendous twenty-volume leatherette-bound
Encyclopedia Britannica
With annually updated fact-files
Guaranteed to the year 2095 A.D.

What has happened? What has happened to us all?
What's happened to the promise of youth? Those dreams?

All of them now seem to be protected
By neighbourhood watch
And are contained within the borders
Of well-trimmed lawns
With little white picket triple-K security fences,
Or parked in double-locked garages
Next to Volvos with solid warrantees

Like so many worn-out slumbering stupid
Down-at-heel floppy hushpuppies.

What's happened to our hopes and dreams?
Those wonderful drug-induced hallucinations
Of our high school years?
God damn those flamingos.
Those bloody pink plastic flamingos.

I think it had something to do with the career counsellors.
All that advice about being sensible at high school.
About being responsible. Being caring and nice.
Nice. Yes. Nice, particularly, has a lot to answer for.

Nice is the best way to kill off the angels in us all.

Those grasping, selfish angels we all were in our youth. >>>

Those inspired angels who told us
To live now and for ourselves. They were killed off.
So, instead we lived for someone else,
And never got around to living for ourselves.

Let's face it. We have demonized
The wrong people over the decades.
Our woes are not due to the family values
Of Charles Manson,
But the diabolical family values of Nancy Reagan.

The time has come to stand up and say 'No!'
Just stand up every time you see a pink flamingo
And shout 'No!'

Write it on a banner in the sky.
Our slogan, our motto, our mantra,
Brothers and Sisters, shall ever after be:

JUST SAY 'NO' TO FAMILY VALUES!
JUST SAY 'NO' TO FAMILY VALUES!
JUST SAY 'NO' TO FAMILY VALUES!

Repeat it, chant it, live it!
And we shall climb the mountain, Brothers and Sisters.
And from the top of the mountain
We shall see a new world dawning.
A new world. And we shall overcome.
Yes. We shall overcome!

Let us take that first step
Against the armies of the moral majority.
That first step is the hardest.
Go ahead. I'll be right behind you.

Sure I will. Go on.

O.K. — You first.

James Deahl

Ulysses

> *The universe is made of stories,*
> *not of atoms.*
> — Muriel Rukeyser

When Ulysses grew frail he lived in Parsons,
on the second floor of a rest home.
On all sides Monongahela National Forest
swept over ridge after ridge of West Virginia.
Blackgum, stave oak, sourwood
flamed up in mixed stands:
a searing red and orange as the frost
came heavy to the hill country.

King of Ithaca, mighty warrior
of Trojan battles, how then is this sick,
old man Ulysses? Ah, grandfather,
your depleted bones and black lungs
have betrayed you into the hands
of nurses, of doctors too young, perhaps,
to understand a miner's pride.

But in your green season, you rose in the dark
to light fire where fire had died,
calling flames from roses of death
to warm the home, heat water for washing.
A wife and eight children up near Chestnut Ridge.

Then out into autumn paths emblazoned
by scarlet hands of sourwood, burning lobes
of blackgum, from every tree a song of birds
heading south . . .

Finally, to end alone in Parsons wondering
whose lungs you can use to breathe,
whose throat to sing.

Confronting The Idea Of The Good On A Rainy Night In Early May

We should have known
during those dark years of Vietnam
America's democracy had ended,
that all our used-up ghosts
were leaving the vacant mills along the Mon.
Tonight, freight cars lurch
where a rail line used to run;
the old marsh returns
making a place a heron might walk
if only in dream.

The rains won't relent.
I will see my parents' graves
and the home where they raised me
never again.
And they were good Presbyterians.
They voted Republican
every other November,
never once failed to keep the Sabbath,
tried to make me into the man
I should have been.

What can we do with the rain?
Looking back half a century
I still can't tell
what I could have done.
Despite this cold Canadian spring
our mulberry finds the strength
to put forth fresh leaves, our lilac prepares
to bloom. I know
beauty to be good; my wife, a good woman.
Across the river: the dead nation of my birth.

Silence In The Fields Of Autumn

So everything is grief
until the green leaves come.
    — Yoshida Kenko

The harp of rain falls quiet.
Drifted maple leaves form a city of light
spread within the shadows
of a copper beech.
Last summer's insects,
like all true nomads,
have gone; only silence remains.

I enter the city of light
where grass leans into winter.
When I look at my hand
I see fields that go on forever,
a distant sea too far away to know.

If I stand here all afternoon
dusk will enter my body,
mix with my blood
to awaken the heart's sorrow.
By then no one will be able to resist
the flute coming down from the mountains.

It is an old friend I had almost forgotten
returning after many years
in this season of need.

Stewart Donovan

In Memory of Seamus Heaney, 1939-2013

He disappeared when children were returning
        to school, waiting with patience in the chariot
we all must ride. The heart gave out sending rich
        ancestral blood to four corners of a temple,
self-fashioned *Grianán of Aileach*. Was there a Polish
        nurse nearby? She would have shown ease with
this patient poet. He was never shy of strangers.
        The day of his death was a warm Irish day.

The harvest has begun here in the Maritimes.
        Now each of us, for whom poetry matters,
reflect on who he was. Pulling slim, dog-eared
        volumes from knapsacks and shelves, digging
words and phrases shaped from Greeks, Saxons,
        Mad Sweeny amid his trees. The boy who
won the Latin prize happiest in fields and soggy fens,
        true archeologist, rain and fog companions
and friends: time traveler in a *teileafón* Tardis he
        should have been a Dublin Dr Who.
The day of his death was a warm Irish day.

He lived in the south but his true measure came
        from the north. Knew his songs would
have to be sung amid suffering. Out of the muck
        of bigotry, bog oak as hard as briar, reclaimed,
refashioned into heirlooms and keepsakes worthy
        of *Ard Rí,* Donegal Drontheim builders,
buskers at the Guildhall. Lights along the Foyle
        shine out for a long-boat to take him in
the wake of *Colm Cille* to Islay, the twin peaks
        of Jura, blue, purple in the far from Greencastle
on a clear Inishowen day. Perhaps. Better maybe
        to see him in Derry, in Badger's below
the wall, nursing a pint before last call.

The Sea Air at Middlehead
>*i.m. John James (Jack) Doucette 1889-1956*
>*Gassed and wounded at the Battle of Arras, Vimy,*
>*1917, with the 85th Battalion, Nova Scotia Highlanders*

After the battle of Arras you wore rags round your eyes,
>Jack, marching blindfolded from Vimy as if to

execution, not in Singer Sargent's *Gassed*, those are Brits
>and Johnny-come-lately-Yanks, for the endgame of 18.

Canadians fought long before, forever in the shadows now,
>forever frozen in time with wounds and froth corrupted

lungs. In countless cenotaphs they hitch up their bronze capes,
>steady their frightened horses, roll their great guns.

Did you romance Mary Helen with your days in France?
>Deracinated Acadian Catholic, unlike the Irish and the

Mik'maq you could imagine fighting *pour les ancêtres,*
>*pour les vieilles cousines qui sont mortes depuis longtemps.*

The fairytale land of Longfellow, Borden and bronzed Evangeline.

The Road to the Keltic Lodge of Corson, Rubber Barron,
>Akron, Ohio, his consumptive wife a patient of faraway spas, come from

away her delicate compromised lungs too bruised
>to be saved by the air of Ingonish and those old friends who sent her

North of Smokey — the legendary Bells of Baddeck,
>Alexander the great: his phones, planes and hydrofoils

mothballed now for museum shelves, school children, tourists.
>Unlike Gatsby (that other great) his dominion over land, sea,

and air outlasted life, but labour leader MacLachlan
>(fellow Scot) would see the science as non-enlightened, corrupted

in the service of capital: machines for the military state
>of what is present, passing and to come.

None of this mattered to you, Jack, as you and your schoolteacher
>bride boarded the *Aspy* for Boston only to return on the tide

to work the short-lived gypsum mine in our baby badlands
>then, in a few desperate breaths, consumption sent you

packing, an inmate of old Point Edward, TB stigmata on your
>battered lungs of Arras, long since beyond the reach of the

air of Ingonish, or the peace of Greencove.

G. W. Down

Trolling Toward Terror

The north men tested their tackle of late.
They lobbed a trap-line, readied a dread reel;
Beware, for the big fish might take the bait.

Repose in the doldrums can dissipate,
And cause calm waters to lose their appeal;
The north men tested their tackle of late.

The lure of game can make some salivate,
Ignore the peril pinned minnows can feel.
Beware, for the big fish might take the bait.

Barbs carelessly launched tend to escalate
Disdain, with foolishness not brought to heel;
The north men tested their tackle of late.

A strike at the hook could precipitate
A cataclysmic wave, an upturned keel;
Beware, for the big fish might take the bait.

Pursuit of such tactics may propagate
Destruction from an overflowing creel.
The north men tested their tackle of late.
Beware, for the big fish might take the bait.

Gertrude Olga Down

Babelplatz, Berlin

At the centre of the Platz
the grey path dissolves to air.
Sunk into the stone, a window
reflects the spire and cupola
of church and university,
reveals submersed chamber that holds
the memory of one frenzied night
when men, eyes poisoned by green lies,
tossed words onto a blazing pyre.
On this square roasted writing of
the dangerous: Dostoevsky,
Ben Franklin, Hegel and Mann,
educators and believers,
philosophers and inventors.
Here the manic's thoughts melted
and all reason burned and curled.
Here, one night papered a crazed world
in rambling clouds of sooty ash —
choked it with forgetfulness.

There is no marker, no plaque,
no words to explain nor redeem.
Only this crypt filled with shelves
empty and silent as dust.

Jennifer Lynn Dunlop

Blue Delphiniums

I planted blue delphiniums
for you
bittersweet sentries

I will sustain them
as I could not sustain you

within them you are suspended
in perennial grace

light caught
in purple curves

life reborn
in soft green lines

fenced in - *Debbie Okun Hill*

Bernadette Gabay Dyer

In the Aftermath

Our names are secret,
Even from the man from Zaire
Who stealthily watches our gestures,
Our moving lips,
And hears our words tangled with sounds
That barricade and isolate, rich with a familiar
Unfamiliar.
And we will not let him in
Until we hear him, and no longer fear him,
His presence brings news from our ancestral home.
His voice is soft,
It cascades as gently as petals,
Then meets with silences
As haunting as the dark stretches of water
Which separate our continental births,
Waters that divide us from her, our mother Africa,
Who is ripe, maternal and calling,
Weary from waiting and wanting
To suckle and nurture us, "her outside children"
Who reciprocate her longings
To fill emptiness in our hearts, our souls,
And she is unmindful of the Jewish, East Indian,
Chinese and European blood
Which over the passage of years
Jostles for attention
In our dark blue veins
Like interconnecting rivers
Where latent memories once shared
Lie buried in a cup of tears.

Where Sunlight Dare Not Follow

The tattoo artist's children
Ungainly tattered
Shiver in coats and ragged boots
As they roam the streets by dark,
Eyes heavy with fire
Rib cages smouldering,
And in the beat of a heart
They are set to running
On their bare feet
That race the wind, regardless of weather,
Their hats pulled down
To shade eyes against sleep,
Against the dark needle's thrill
As joyously they chase dogs tails
Through alleys and lanes
Where sunlight dare not follow,
The melancholy artist's daughters and wayward sons
Flash bright smiles that crack gaping holes in their jaws
To mark them indelible
Like their blue veined rememberings
Of indigo ink
That still lives
In the silky white of their skin

Margaret Patricia Eaton

Sunflowers

No shy violets here, or exotic orchids,
no greenhouse nurturing,
no modest draping of bronze bellies
swollen with seed life.

These are living stone fertility goddesses,
rooted in the Earth,
turning to worship the Sun-God Ra,
their wanton gold petals glowing
and dancing in his light,

embodying the spirit of Eternal Woman,
earthy,
nourishing,
primeval,
indestructible.

Winter Woods

A glittering surface beckons
before diamond crust gives way
to knee-deep powder.
Marshmallow-coated spruce needles
offer sharp rebuff.
Nothing is what it seems.

Tree skeletons hold life secrets
in rings within rings,
patterns copied from planets' paths,
sacred circles of memories
remapped by shape-shifters,
dream catchers.

In winter woods
unshaven alder bristles
poke through snow-skin
while amid January's iron-grip
water flows under ice.

Ronda Wicks Eller

Prostrate in Byzantium

I remember Paris, France —
the gentle sheeting of rain
sheening on the window pane
and glistening heated flesh entwined,
refusing rest beneath the lamplight glow,
rapt in some penultimate dance;
the only one we were ever meant to know.

And there we held our suspect hearts
firm, scarce of breath, in absolute union,
paralyzed, yet in total effusion
and somehow fully dancing still.

We lay prostrate in Byzantium,
too proud to sacrifice ambition
for judicial writ or ordination
and so, no golden chalice sipped,
no wedding feast or ringing bell —
just the creaking of a caster bed
to consecrate our ritual.

Daniela Elza

autobiography of grief   1

the copper snowflakes.
      the broken boat in which
we sleep   with our backs to each other.

self portrait with bird.   replicated.
over and over —   a vow

      cast in the heaviest steel
at the centre   of our room.

        there is no parting —

in the latest unfinished sentence
the image floats   homeless
    until   someone walks away.

church bells   briefly disperse   the noise
of the city —

    a city hammered out of copper
and clay.   each morning
    snapped tight on the forehead.

feet nailed to a floor they know too well.

        each day
  an altar in the corner burns
hope
as if it were lamp oil.

Joseph A. Farina

morning essence

7 a.m.
on a cold November
the sun has not risen
the darkness still owns us
outside in the pre-dawn
spirits are waiting
i hear them like music
stirring my soul
shivering in silence
i turn and remember
a scene set in sadness
much like this darkness
in a sterile room holding
the shell of my maker
while i in my numbness
held on to his hand
cold as this morning's light
first kiss on the land —
you were not there
but i know that you felt it
the whispers of mornings'
call to surrender
with professional mercy
they put him to rest
and sometimes in mornings
before light embraces
the hopes of the living
when we are driving this highway
near dawn
i sense someone tending
through clouds and dark shadows
sojourners among us
between darkness and light

Venera Fazio

Broken
    In memory of Zio Carlo Fazio (1922-1969)

A snake
skin of ebony
mirrors
shimmering Sicilian sun
stretches
across your tombstone.

While you were alive
we locked your name
in our family closet
sealed it shut with silence.

Decades later
from cracked seal
seeped sibling stories:
your rages
quickness with switch blade
suicide attempt
in the reservoir of Cootes Paradise.

Then, confinement in Hamilton Sanatorium.
The skipped medical payments
your deportation back to ageing parents
and early death by pneumonia
in archaic Messina hospital.

Before the war
Carlo was molto bravo
lamented a sister.
He suffered a brain injury
falling off an army truck
said one brother, not convinced.
Another brother declared
No, no, he was broken . . .
days trapped in a sewer.
Someone snitched and the Germans
bombed the hideout.
Your uncle was the only survivor.

The snake snaps open his jaws
points unfurled fangs
towards me.
Can only the living
fully forgive each other?

Point of Departure, 1951

For my passport picture
I wear wedding dress
soft gingham, lace collar.
I look through the camera
into the future
with Rosario
sweet mannered, gentle
waiting for me in Canada
with pick and shovel
crushing quarry stones
into weekly salary.

I discard
mother-in-law
who withholds love
although I trudge miles
under a punitive sun
gathering wood to stoke bread oven.

Away from Sicily
I will loosen
parental knot of shame
twisted tight by my father
whenever he betrays my mother, bedding her sister
and neglects Santa and Emilio, cousins/half-brother and
sister.
To quell my cousins' hollow cries of hunger
I fill their pockets with handfuls of chick peas and
almonds.

Fran Figge

The Fault of the Apple

Cradled in the thighs of a branch, blushing flesh
sways in the humid swell of air,
innocent illumination exposing
her flawless first flush.
Dewdrop-slicked ripe curves
tempt him.

With sibilance of slithering, leathery skin
slides over her smoothness
aching for a taste.
Forked tongue flicking reticent flesh, laps
the bitter-sweet tang of her nectar.

Coiled in embrace,
he calms her quivering trepidation,
his length hardening
as he pierces her resistance.

A red stain blooms on her white core,
seeds of life and death laid bare.

Expended in *la petite mort*, he sleeps
beside her plumped softness,
breathing the musk of satisfaction
and her dream-drenched sighs.

Eyes open to the new dawn, light unveiling
a lusty promise —
the fresh allure of more fruit —
unspoiled.

Doris Fiszer

In the Year Before She Died

Two dreams over and over.
First she left my brother and me
in front of the mall, waved,
drove off.

In the other she and I stood
in front of my childhood cottage
— its orange shutters, tire swing,
stork statue in the front yard —
everything the same.

By the water Mother warned
don't swim out too far,
walked away, didn't look.

In hospital she stared
at her frozen arm and leg,
mouth and tongue
twisted familiar words,
refused the ice chips I offered.

Night blurs.
In sleep she's here,
opens her arms to me.

Foraging

i

From mid May to late October
especially after heavy rain
we head to the Gatineau woods
carrying baskets, paring knives,
whistles around our necks —
to scare off bears
or blow hard if we get lost.

Father in the lead, my mother, brother
and I struggling to keeping pace.
Slow down, my mother yells
but he keeps running,
only stopping briefly to look
under and around each tree
for gold in the forest.

Sometimes we hike for hours without luck
on rare occasions, rewarded
with a never-ending sea
of yellow chanterelles or elusive morels.

We set each gem carefully in our basket.

At home we devour some sautéed boletes
in butter with onions and scrambled eggs
for a late lunch.

ii

My mother and I work fast
to dehydrate the rest while they are fresh.

We clean each one gently
with a small soft brush, separate
stem from cap, place them on foil-lined racks
in a slow oven,

turn them after an hour,
let them slowly dry for another.

The scent of drying fungi
lingers in the kitchen for days.

We fill air tight glass jars
with shrivelled pieces,
store the jars on basement shelves beside mushrooms pickled
in white vinegar, black peppercorns and onions.

Rehydrated, they make their way
into Mother's goulash, chicken and dumpling soup,
sauerkraut and mushroom pierogi.

My father told us to downplay
our bounty's size
to their Polish friends if they inquired

to never reveal our prime sites.
We could disclose our gutted locations
or ones where no mushrooms grew.

Isn't that lying? I ask.

Mushroom hunting is a competitive sport
my mother says.
*All Polish parents train their children
in the same way.*

iii

I've lost the certainty
of identifying edible mushrooms
just as I've lost the certainty
of some childhood memories.
No one in my family is left who can help me.

My dried mushrooms come from Costco
a tall plastic container —
yellow boletes, oysters, porcinis and portobellos.

Infused in hot water, then added
to turkey soup, slow-cooking stew
and spaghetti sauce.

Each time I open the jar
I see my mother sitting at her kitchen table
an overflowing bushel of chanterelles before her.

Kate Marshall Flaherty

Lost

I once learning the word
migwetch
in a place of sweet grass
and sunlight

I felt many earth-words —
the drumming pound,
Manitoulin sand packed
beneath our feet

a circle of fancy dance
and jingle jumps
rejoicing

recalling how women
were the first drummers
plucking beats
out of needle and hoop
quill, skin

I had a drum teacher once
long ago, we all did
in the womb

fire earth wind
singing like water
timbrel and tongue

cedar boughs on poles
to shade our tender white skin
gifts we were given
of cloth and craft

the book of strawberry stories
and a ladybug
medicine wheel

the hush of a dropped eagle feather

my boys chasing
children into the schoolhouse

serious laughter
cedar tea and *migwetch*
every summer

Jennifer L. Foster

Wild Apple Tree

Inside
an apple's core
a ghostly orchard stirs
by crimson harvest moon cajoled
to seed

In Snug Harbour, Georgian Bay

Rough pine door, ajar,
freshly smoked whitefish on racks
a spiral of gulls

Quiet before the storm - *Richard M. Grove*

Linda Frank

A Long Time Coming

Spring eddied beneath the wind that week
in the mountains, and the rains came
off and on, but in between the sky cleared,

a sharp Dresden blue, and along the Bow River,
something brought the sudden smell of salt, memory
of another spring and its smudged cobalt sky.

And though for weeks I'd held myself closed,
for one small moment, I listened to the beat
of my heart, and in the night, insomnia came

again, perched outside my window
with the mountains and the moon, and the blues
came down hard and for days I let them
      come.

There's a current that rides the night winds
in Banff. A danger in the bowl of mountains.
And one night that week I had the taste

of salt on my tongue when I went to see a band
play the blues in the Rundle Lounge of the Banff Springs
Hotel, all the lights turned up high and bright, people

coming and going, no one listening to them and I knew
it was only the scotch in my glass, the beat
of my heart, the moon and the mountains that night,

knew that's all it was. But when the singer covered
Sam Cooke, sang as if change was really gonna come,
for one small moment I wanted to believe it was true,

though I knew it wasn't. You and me, we'd never change,
and the truth had been a long time coming. And the blues
came down hard that night, came down hard. And
      I let them come

Chasing Shadows

Most nights she lies on her back in her darkened
bedroom — head, arms and legs spread

out in a five point star, floating
between the stereo speakers. Floating

      on a mobius strip of Chicago blues, a white
suburban kid drifting and drifting inside The Resurrection
of Pigboy Crabshaw, Paul Butterfield's harp

a vibrato wind coming up before a storm. Elvin Bishop's
guitar bending the notes like someone walking

      alone in the night, bending
                to that wind.

When the band comes to town, playing six nights
in a row at the New Penelope, she's underage,

but she sneaks in every one of those nights to hear the blues
played live. And she's young, yes, but the minor notes
take her wild, touch down deep in her

and that week the band has a guy not much older than she is
sitting in, playing harp.
              Will Scarlett. It's the best name
she's ever heard and after they play their last song

she goes home and lies awake all night, drifting and drifting,
      a ship out on the sea, she and Will.

                She's a rider by his side.

You've Been On My Mind

Perhaps it's the fate of the yellow
chrysanthemum so arresting
in my October garden
that places you
here on my mind
when I will not place you
in my life

Or the shock of yellow marigolds
I've gathered for my windowsill
that tells me
how I can not
gather your body
in my arms
Maybe it's the mark of yellow
dust from anthers
pregnant with pollen
staining my fingertips
that reminds me of how
I will not allow
my hands
to touch you

This yellow
arrived so late
in my fall garden
This yellow
bursting
from darkness

Ryan Gibbs

Daylight my Darknesses
    for Ray Souster

Riding a thundering horse
down Dundas and Elizabeth,
the banker sought inspiration
in the unspoken courage of
the girls at the corner.

He went back for Gwen
but never found her,
only stories that
she too was lost,
in some mad search
for stray alley cats.

What he discovered
was poetry
as elusive as
Queen Anne's Lace,
tiny prayers of comfort,
as he prepared for
a final journey
into darkness

totem - *David Haskins*

65

Sharon Goodier

Nothing Left Behind
    after the Fort McMurtry fire summer 2016

apocalyptic fire
everything abandoned
except dignity

glimpse of end times
stripped of property
persona

what's real is
all that remains
essential

the core of our humanity
no I am or I have
just an embrace of emptiness

absence of things
we thought mattered
a fullness of faith. Hope

and the love of strangers

Katherine L. Gordon

Leonardo's Flying Machine
    as seen modeled at Montreal Museum

The longing overwhelmed me
when I saw it,
as it must have possessed Leonardo,
the time-traveler whose spirit could leap
outside the confines of the medieval mind
to fly into a universe of thought,
where man could soar with birds
in a light canvas-on-wood
swallow-tailed, one-with-the-air frame,
catch the updraft
glide over green spaces
close the eyes and inhabit the wind.

He comes through the centuries
as I touch his machine
built to tantalize the earth-bound.
I want to devour the grace,
the hurtful beauty
of a glider born
to bridge not only man and bird,
but free the soul,
lift you over the torpid,
no fire, no sound,
a kite into eternity.

Beowulf's Blade

Beowulf is in those woods
where the mists writhe,
he has taken his sacred weapon
from the great hall
and written my name on its blade.
Where time-strings collide
in dark November thickets
I am drawn to test the walls
between the circles of creation.
Rain-bells glisten like fairy globes
on the tips of black-laquered branches,
radiant witnesses to the stealthy unraveling
of all the runes and riddles
that have prophesied this time.
All the summers of opiate denial,
soul-sleeps of winter,
fevers of spring,
have been stage curtains
for November's grave-goods galliard.
Fear and longing collide in this dance
as I turn alone to call his name,
one must slay the unholy parts,
wake to other partners.

Elizabeth Greene

Reading Ivy Compton-Burnett

Turning the pages of *Manservant and Maidservant*
I think of Max White, monklike, in his basement apartment,
eyes large behind cataract glasses, arthritic hands
gnarled around his chair or cane or glass,
steps slow, but words winged, flying with a freedom
denied his body.
                        One vodka-soaked afternoon
he said, *Read Ivy Compton-Burnett*.
I gazed at the photographs of puppets in his bookcase,
at the Alice Neel painting of a child alone in a grey room
with one small window. Max reached for the Stolichnaya
and our glasses. Why Ivy Compton-Burnett?

I tried to search her books out, couldn't find them.
For years I didn't even try.

Now, inside her pages, I spell out between lines
wrung from day after changeless day,
in the novels and in her writing life,
the calm after the relentless tragic years when father,
brothers, sisters, mother died.

Max White must have known
what I could learn from these quiet novels,
her happy endings: absence of change.
Her accomplishment: catching voices,
biting words — characters staving
off disaster for another year.

Andreas Gripp

The West Coast of Somewhere

As a boy, I saw only sand and sea
and stones I pitched with a splash
beneath the shifting animal clouds
that I envisioned.

As a single young man
on a day of sun and cirrus,
I knew nothing of rocks
and waves colliding with the shore,
only the flash of skin and curves
exposed for browning.

Now middle-aged in wedlock,
ambling along the beach
beside my wife,
I see the patterns on pebbles
and the gulls that dip for trout
while the crew of college girls,
jumping for *frisbees* in the surf,
are supposedly a blur below
this cumulus of savannah cats
overseeing their great,
ephemeral kingdom.

Marooning the Muse
for Carrie

We sat at the beach together
but I didn't write a thing.
I looked to the horizon
and its meeting of sky and sea
and the cerulean they both shared
at the point where we see
the world is round indeed.

You wrote of sandpipers
on the strand and the seagulls
encircling the trawler
traversing the harbour,

and I left you the metaphors
to find while I was lost in a reverie
that had Magellan meeting
Eratosthenes
on the edge of a precipice,
saying yes, it's all an illusion,
this vortex of birds and their fish,
this looping of ships and our poems.

Richard M. Grove

Aching to be On the Water, March 22

With morning blur I look past
burgundy blooms of my re-flowering orchid
to motionless grey branches.
Red-winged blackbirds and finches arrived last week.
As if in a panic, dogs barking at my heels, fire lapping,
I rummage for my life jacket. With a shrill
I blew the cobwebs from my emergency whistle,
grabbed my toque and gloves and headed to wake
my kayak from a five month slumber.

Scratched over winter's dirty gravel shore,
I slip her belly into freezing lake,
skimming to freedom.
Cornflake size, fluffy flakes, parachute through
sullen sky, freckling
mirrored cove, melting
on bobbing green prow.

It is well past middle March
but still there were crystals of ice
on south shore hidden
in deep shadows, death clinging
to last year's rushes.

I paddled first into calm
testing my steel.
With gained confidence I headed north
past the tip of Salt Point into waves
of an east wind pushing quickening foam
over bow. I zipped my collar
tight, snugged the straps of my life jacket,
tilting my strokes towards lighthouse.
Gloved fingertips now wet and freezing,
lap splashed, bobbing wildly
in troughs of black.
I swing east around Boulder Island,
I sing west, surfing,
by wind and waves, south back
into the leeside calm of the cove.
As I drag my kayak from lapping shore
placed back into its bed of crunching leaves
my spirit sings.

David Haskins

Resilience
    for Robert Davidson, Haida Master Carver, and painter of The Southeast Wind.

    . . . and hope that the stories that live inside the curl of your knuckles
    can be coaxed out one more time
        - Richard Wagamese, 2015 Matt Cohen Award Speech

How do you paint the Southeast wind
that blows the pox into every eye
turns villages to burial grounds and topples totems
crashes warriors in a foamy stew
carries off children to an alien language
churns the gravel in the salmon creek beds
and cracks the canoe inside the tree?

You pound the red ochre to powder
mix salmon eggs with your spit
take thirty seconds to doodle a design
and one whole day to crisp a line
where negative is positive is negative again
the need for yes or no forgotten on the wind
that lifts the killer whale light as air.

Wind moves the line, line leads the eye
eye guides the hand, hand cuts the curve;
charcoal blackens thick skeletal bones
around u-shaped fins, ovoid head,
blowhole, teeth, tail, eye already human;
formlines winnow, dissipate energy
away from the dematerialized numinous beast.

                                                            >>>

The storm drum beats on top of Tow Hill.
The spirit creature breaches from a crack in the past
when the door between worlds was easily opened.
Grab the wind by its kelp hair, pull it into your canoe.
Paint the Southeast, and his mother, Tomorrow;
Paint your people's journey through storm and sorrow.
Look back where you came from, then walk a new path.

All that remains are moss covered thresholds,
green indentations in the forest floor,
a mortuary board, a potlatch pole leaning
and elders' stories ten thousand years old.

I sit with a Watchman on a log in South Moresby
the morning fog shrouding the silent sea.
He shares his breakfast with a deer at arm's length
and turns his face to the Southeast wind.

NOTE: *Robert Davidson is one artist who has brought back to his people their culture, stories, myths, their identity, names, spirituality, their pride and dignity. He has shown them where they came from, and what they had taken from them — their potlatches, language, children, and 90% of their people. Under the tutelage of master carvers Charles Edenshaw and Bill Reid, and filtering traditional techniques and forms through his unique imagination, he paints the Southeast wind as its transformative spirit being, the killer whale.*

Reclamation

He was the first to build a picture window
shear off trees
leaving the tangling roots.
He trimmed the greening earth
and ferreted out weeds
with methodical madness.
The wire-worms slipped deeper down their black holes.

Some white days the lake became sky
and his world stopped at the cliff edge.
The water sucked sand
from under his feet
stole beneath the slope
cracked the surface
and a piece of his world was space.

On limpid winter nights
he slid down the ice banks
while the swells slapped below
like a father admonishing an infant.
What stars,
silent eyes in a midnight forest,
plotted his possibilities?

He moved his chair to the centre of the room
when the wave gathered
like legions on the horizon line
rolling high over the water
a raw emerald curl
swallowing beach and cliff
crashed upon the window

and receded
dropping grey-white mountains on his lawn.
The second ice-blue force
smashed the glass
and spent its last upon his eyes.
Quiescent
he waited for the ice to come.

Rhoda Hassmann

Bronze-Skinned Woman

I don't talk about it much,
she says:
Some people were child soldiers
some worked in the fields

I saw murders
with spades, axes, bare hands;
Children killing their parents
each other

People executed
for scrounging fruits and bugs and roots
skin flaked and dulled to gray
hair uncombed by decree

I've been so lucky, she says
pulling her orange shawl tight around her shoulders
Everybody's so good to me in America;
I'm married too, and have a baby

I don't talk about it with my husband
we just talk about household stuff
and my father fell apart after we came here
so I don't talk to him either

I was a child slave
It's too personal
to talk about

Between Massacres
South Africa, August 1992

In this land stretched taut and flat,
soil so thin, you can hear the ground underneath
screaming for relief, and the gold mine scars
weeping to be closed

A tourist hires a guide to take her
one thousand kilometers
to see one particular ostrich

I saw lots, on the way to Fort Hare
ostriches as big as cows, blending in the barrens
past the barren squatted yards
of the townships, and the long open fields
filled with outhouses, waiting for the blacks
to move in from the drought

They give them pit latrines
now that freedom's coming

Debbie Okun Hill

An Old Miner's House

You remind me of a weathered boot
with a worn out sole, droopy eyelets,
and a mouse squeak left abandoned
near a shut-down silver mine.

I became the mother
who moved in from the cold
cooked wild rabbit and squirrel
raised children in this shoe.

Today, there are gardeners
who recycle leathered goods,
fill each cavity with dirt,
and plant a prickly plant inside.

I wished to be *aloe vera* juice:
someone to heal your heart,
breathe fresh air into your curtains,
and soothe all that ailed you.

Your advanced age should have softened
your hard corners, removed
the stubbornness, and sanded-down
the edge in your creaky voice.

You are an old house but you held me close:
taught me lessons at a slower pace,
showed me your attic of familial memories,
tied our laces together, and restored

    my faith   in forgotten places.

cut - *Debbie Okun Hill*

Eryn Hiscock

Harem (Ted Bundy Poem)

— In the woods, there are communions
between me and her where I
hardly catch my breath
(and she never catches hers)
yet she keeps resurrecting herself,
and I sacrifice her, and
all her incarnations
as offerings for the beasties
high in the forest
they scatter my brides
like wedding rice.

I return when I can't recognize
anyone anymore,

(she looks all the same
undressed of flesh).

For consummation
I prefer
decay to faces —

morning halos
a skull socket

I watch the sun rise
where her eyes were.

After *Frankenstein*

Stuttering synapses
nerves shuddering
lurching momentum
in fits and starts

Some skeletons
six feet under
are less themselves

With recycled eyes
another life flashes
before his
mishmash
mismatch

all thumbs
and two left feet.

No — really:
Two left feet.

He never meant
to kill anyone

— it's just —

once seized —
again —
with life —

he grips too tight.

Lawrence Hopperton

McCraney

What happens at camp stays at camp

    1

5:30. Coffee and donuts.
Check the trailer, the canoes,
drive north a half hour late
at the ranger station — they don't care.
Launch at Rain Lake, paddle
the narrows. Stern starboard and
the portage is there. Drag the packs

up the embankment, then canoes.
Load up; should be a fairly easy few
kilometers, cart wide, mostly
level. They go to the dam twice a year
through the bush. Walk 10; rest 5.
It's further than you can swat
and when you're done, come back for the rest.

    2

It wasn't like that at all. McCraney
with his bum leg canoes for hours.
He doesn't stop deer flies or mosquitoes.
They bite through the narrows, sweating

paddles-stokes the lake, swing
south; the portage is that way,
as flat as the forest and wide.
Repellant doesn't work. Wet feet,

arms and legs, socks and hiking shoes
packed tight, with hang-ons, dry-bags,
canoes. Your day pack sweats
in your eyes, bleeding in your shirt —

everything out of slapping reach.
"Ouch! My head! Are we there yet?"

>>>

3

One in front. Keep moving.
Rest. Keep moving. Rest.
Your water bottle. Loaded,
launch ahead but nobody said

leeches or this beaver dam.
"McCraney, it's one of your poems!"
Step delicate, slide down easy:
lily-pads, underwater dead

heads and frogs all the way
down. This lake has no reeds
no shallows only driftwood shores.
The dam is closed; fish are deep.

Camp on the east side of the island
sheltered with rods and painted lures
past the cliff with anchoring roots.
Beach, steady. Unload. Steady.

4

You will see stars from here,
fledgling loons, thunder moon,
sunrise trees, the lake laugh,
shoulders glister like muscle

memory flying forward as fast
as a blue canoe can go
past the island all the way.
Bushwhack barefoot if you have to.

We're this close, this back-water bower
painted green with rusts chains, holding
spill-down four meters high. Nothing
too far; white water in town.

Laurence Hutchman

La Dentellière
after Vermeer

Bent over your lace,
everything in your body
draws me toward your hands;
I can feel the tension
as you pull the two strands of thread.

The way you bend is your inclination
to thread the form of fabric.
Your cheeks and hidden smile
(if it is a smile at all)
are directed to the point in the sewing of the blue cloth.

So I observe you
concentrating on the point of that pattern you make.
I feel the motion of your hands, forearms, shoulders
threading your life,
forgetting about children, family, history
weaving them through your hands.

How Vermeer has poised your eloquent fingers,
your needle suspended in perfect tension.
I look at you in that gold and white dress;
the blue fabric is so tactile,
I could run my finger over it.
Lacemaker, you spin fabric out of yourself,
draw me into the flowers of the sun
as you float there
alive to the graceful interaction of work and life . . .

Milkweed

A thirteen-year old boy in the ravine
lifts the milkweed pod through mauve sky upward,
releases seeds to the moon.
        The weed, not flower, not jack-in-the-pulpit,
but rough skin, nodules,
     bumps, hard metacarpal,
        faded puce, mole fur, velvet-ridged, a broken boat.
Once in public school we drew the pod
until it became a thousand things:
a clown striped banana,
a green beaked parrot perched in the wind
or a mouth opening revealing
soft down skin
       with tiny seeds that resembled
delicate Japanese prints.
The pod breaks open, launches its seeds,
humming-bird's tail, comet-blue light . . .
like decorations of an Irish Christmas tree.
When blowing in the wind
they dance, circles rise, spin and drop jazzy rhythms
words . . . rising . . . rushing . . .
     domestic sputniks,
playful gyroscopes
       drifting stars.
At thirteen, I flip open its coarse green-tufted skin
among tall frosted grass
   they float up a ladder of lace,
  space pods
       spiralling through the mist
          toward the moon —
           their own milky way.

Luciano Iacobelli

The Egg Poem

"One singular egg" he said.

"How would you like your egg?" she asked.

"cosmic" he said,

"and if you loved me, you'd lay it yourself.
You'd execute an inner contortion,
an intrauterine utterance perfectly oval,
a vulvic labial expression,
and you'd lay it here on my breakfast plate.

The shell would be so white and strong,
as if somehow you'd recruited the tundra
or knitted together a chainmail of avalanches
to protect the soft inside,
the gooey anarchy.

If you loved me you'd crack open this egg,
(its heart sick of its own self containment)
and you'd let the contents spill;
maybe you could flatten yourself
spread yourself under it like a pan
and fry the egg over easy
with every inch of your being."

"You'd do this if you loved me," he concluded.
She said "but I'm only a waitress taking your order."
"Don't underestimate yourself" he said,
"by your strut alone, it's clear
you're more than you can ever know:
a sacred text written in lipstick Sanskrit,
a universal principal in a tight skirt."

Keith Inman

Glass
      War Remnants Museum, Ho Chi Minh City

People, four and five deep, shuffle
along partitioned
glass panels past photos of the missing
and dead

a photographer's requiem.

A woman ahead of me turns.
Our eyes lock.
Her mouth opens.
She is shaking, her hands
churn in prayer. Silently,

she rejoins the crush
of others, who also turn
to complete strangers

to be sure they aren't alone
in the witness of war,
the breach across a barrier
of black and white.

They are only photos
I tell myself:

a man grimaces at a gun
against the fountain of blood
flowing from his head in a day-lit
street of people looking on;

uniformed boys wallow in waist deep
mud, pulling a brother, a comrade, a son
home, his vacant
glass eyes already there;

a Captain wears a white explosion
as he scrambles forever
in fore-shadowed death. That
one, short, hill behind him;

the back-lit cross of a girl runs naked
beside a grim brotherhood of soldiers
fleeing allied planes, her body
a flame with fallen sky. Tara-Linh

hurries through the exhibit. Waits
for me to pick my way through. We sit
under a staircase window and don't
talk about leaving as light
begins to exit the room
the way security
herds a crowd
toward a door.

Outside, a line of dark clouds surges
toward a stalled sun as tank-rolls of rain
walls off the street.

Shops and palm trees across the road
disappear.

We hold hands, slip
through throngs of tourists
charging for shelter, and make our way
to the back steps
where we sit and stare
at the steaming
drying road
in a sudden sun returned.

No one bothers us.

Lake Fever
Slabtown (Niagara), July 12th, 1849

They swayed in the hard seated cart along
the treelined trail to Welland, horses
knowing the way to a warm stall. Johnny
was just giddy for being alive.

Come up north two years now, got a ride
with the Coloured Corps for his time
hunting buffalo. Sergeant Billie, his brow shining
like a new colt, broke the chitter of birds,
"You thinkin' of going back now word's come up
'bout a relentin?' Johnny smiled, "You mean,
where everything but winter tries to kill you."
Billie laughed, "That's what a women's for.
Though you probably ain't worth even that."

The hot sun beat down on the blue of his rifle,
Johnny let his hand drop. Never
had he seen the likes of a man black as night
tell white folk how things was gonna be. Old Billie,
straight-backed in glowing red serge, hands
glasped in front like he was about to give sermon
with his choir boys shuffling in sole worn boots
behind him as Green and Orange-men whistled
bullets and curses at each other. The Lord knowing
they couldn't tell one from the other.

And the English, set well back up the ridge,
crows waiting for a corn spill as Billie
told the Irish, "Go ahead, kill each other.
There's folks ready to take them starvin'
Rye jobs building this here canal. You
in for haulin' stone, Johnny?" He yelled back,
like Johnny was gonna answer.

A soft patch in the corduroy road jolted him
awake as the land cleared to scrub farm
above the escarpment, where the poor
grew stones for graves in a King's land for order.
Johnny glanced across at Billie,
who was sweating fever.

Susan Ioannou

Mineralogy Lesson

Staring at crystals
this man is a scientist,
and when I murmur of mysteries

"Physics," he grunts.
"Temperature and speed.
That's why a crystal grows, or doesn't."

What a wonder it grows at all!
How hidden under the earth
water, light, and air gather
dendrite on dendrite, facet by facet,
becoming a geometrical bloom,
or soften and redissolve.

He smirks.
"It's ions.
Diffusion."

But I believe:
the inanimate is prickly with soul,
or why do its ions attract, heat rising,
and fasten on others
faster and faster?
Isn't that love?

"It's physics,"
he insists. "Physics."
— unaware he blushes.

Imagine That Greek Island

Half bare on baked white rock
you'd overlook the bay.
The day is hot. Dry light
bronzes your skin
and water's turquoise
blinds, silvered with stars.

Over white stucco and red tiled roofs
a *taverna*'s *clarino* twists on the air.
Hear the shuffle of dancing
— *Kalamatianós, Hasápiko.*
Sniff the sweat and smoke
spitting as *souvlaki* turns.

In your hands
moist vine leaves, plucked
to fold with rice, ground meat,
lemon, and oil, are enough
for lean, rolled-shirtsleeved men
to swallow with *raki*
— their smiles
a foretaste of love
when the sun slips
its bloodied fin
under the wave.

I.B. Iskov

When He Died, He Took One Last Poem with Him
   for Earle Birney

He lived his life like a leaf
dancing and singing
from a hazel bough
in winter, he'd simply move
the tree indoors

His words etched
a million faces on paper
burned a memory in metaphor
cities of parchment
exploded like firecrackers

His hands molded pictures
like a sculptor he'd fashion
shadows in holes
and everyone would gasp
at their exactness

The ritual was a myth

He sleeps with one last poem
as a blanket to cover
the decay of genius
now and forever

Ellen S. Jaffe

Water Children

> *Buddhist women may sometimes have special prayers*
> *and shrines for babies who were aborted, whom they call*
> *"water children."*

I

Water child, I bring you
chrysanthemums, ripe pears,
coloured ribbons to tie up my prayers
You live, still, floating in some sunless sea
out of reach   out of reach
I call you by name, but you
are too far away
and you have not yet learned
how to hear.

II

I am the water child
I am a lump of sugar dissolved in a bowl of green tea
next to these white chrysanthemums and red ribbons
I am a small pool, with one goldfish swimming in circles.
I am a humming-bird's tongue, double-dipped in nectar.
     Do not be sad
     I am not angry at you
     See — I will kiss you there, there
     Nectar-wet kisses so another child
     Can begin
My kiss is a tiny moth,
a mayfly that lives only one day.
Someday you will forget me
but not yet, not now
     I need to water the white chrysanthemums
     I need the red ribbon connecting us, heart to heart
     as it did once
     while I lay sleeping underwater, inside your skin.

III

I will sing you a lullaby,
braid the prayer-ribbons, red and green,
around this pear.
You could be the child inside the peach-pit
who accomplishes great deeds,
kills the raging monsters causing havoc
     in the kingdom of my dreams.
Timimoto, Tom Thumb, Thumbelina
     my bushel of tears   my water child.

Another Kind of War Story
a response to Adrienne Rich's poem "Rape,"
in Diving into the Wreck, 1973

You remember the policeman in your kitchen,
the night it happened,
how his gaze
flicks from you to the poster of Ho Chi Minh
with its delicate poem about peace
on a wall the colour of ripe papaya.

When he looks at you again,
you are more the enemy, less the victim.

You remember the doctor, emergency-called
that Friday evening, telling you
you'd be fine to wait until after the weekend.

You find another doctor.

Even now, more than forty years later,
as you lie in bed with your lover,
dappled in morning sun, you remember

that classroom on Mulberry Street in New York,
rainy afternoon after school,
teenage boy with his red pen-knife,
later stabbed
by a vigilante gang
for shaming the neighbourhood,

and the male policeman in your clean kitchen,
tucking your underwear into a plastic bag
as he asks about the boy's identity, his race
shadowed by a poster from a war
(not) so far away.

Carol Keller

Dirty Love

Motor oil, grime, grease
The smell of care, strength
endurance, provision.

Mechanical repair wiped away
Clean skin and hair
shed grains of hardened rust
that's been jarred, hammered
bent and torqued.

A shop full of labour
Fatigue's odour on
muscled forearms
scarred with burns
Chinks of routed skin
that got in the way.

The slip of the vise
The grip loosened
The broken bolt
The fearsome swearing
That accompanies pain.

This is dirty love
Not a well dressed preacher,
playing with words,
Or a well dressed teacher
wiping minds with a
dry erase brush.

Old Quebec City - *David Haskins*

Eva Kolacz

Inquiry into Pastoral Life

> *Nobody can bring you peace but yourself.*
> \- Ralph Waldo Emerson

    I

Let's have dreams
blooming, ripe with fruit which will not be
the subject of a future recall.
Meet me ex-urbanite, who left the smog & traffic of Toronto
for pastoral life (no, not exactly — farm animals
are hardly seen here)
only their shadows dance, jump & shine with ease.
Change becomes us — someone said.
The beginning leaves the past behind.
This is what a poet & mystic can define
effortlessly.

On the rooftop
crows sampling the air under their wings
& swearing in harsh tones
at my unfamiliar face.

    II

Mad, mad heat has put the month of August on the grill,
fields of corn exploding with fire,
sky is dry & exhausted
making the days shrink and disappear.
Last night I cut up photographs.
Departing has the taste of sadness
the thread is a broken   connection lost   a piece of ash.

A few memories will reappear again
in our sleep by using camouflage to hide their apparent meaning
& wake us up.
Some will turn their faces away from you
and on some you will turn your back.

Maureen Korp

Friday afternoon

camera crews here, there
tracking telephoto lens
sirens, noises, cries

raucous, crackling shrieks
somatic witness, skin stripped
raw. All gone wrong

gunmen in the mosque
men with bandoliers, and prayers . . .
bullets.　here.　　young men

with guns, laden with
grenades. Soon the bodies stink
on rugs laid out for

prayer. The arguments
of faith, dismembered reason
flayed, drained dry, giddy

in the summer's heat,
blackbirds, crows wheel about
who will pray for what

Laurie Kruk

Birds of America
    for Cynthia Sugars

    Audubon, loving that rich land as few men have loved it,
    before or since, captured within his books, and saved for
    us who must painfully correct our ancestors' mistakes,
    the essence of America that was.

        - William Vogt, Introduction, *The Birds of America;*
                                          9th ed. (1971)

Two things, John James Audubon —
Haitian-born *Rabin*, bastard self-inventor,
American woodsman who wrapped himself first
in bear grease, then mystique of the Lost Dauphin —
especially envies them: their song and
        flight. Taking subscriptions
from titled Europeans or colonial bourgeoisie
for his monument, *Birds of America,*
he abandons his family, wife, lover, seeks passage on boats
from the Florida everglades
where he cages and kills the Golden Eagle,
to the desolate outcrops of Labrador
in search of the Great Auk, already almost mythical
as it entered his pages
which he cannot stop filling,
because no matter his dissection, he cannot divine how they
        soar. Nor wrestle
the golden notes from emptied throats
with his love of art, passion for
discovery, after the fact: in water and oils. Wired
in place, Audubon's birds
are painted onto pastoral backdrops
where voices, wings are stilled and colours fade.

                                                                              >>>

As images, they embody the lesson of chromatics:
truth that we are receivers only, given sight
to register sums of orange, blue, red, teal, scarlet —
       only sometimes given vision.
Meanwhile, Audubon's birds became
puppets of themselves,
portraits purchased by armchair explorers
and penitent capitalists, finally elevated into
idols of The Audubon Society, dedicated to
conservation, as their namesake was
to preservation, providing this paradox:
       To kill the thing
you love, or love
       the thing you kill?

His passionate attention to detail
condemns them to paper cages,
while his winged brush dances
       finally free —
Piercing his prey through the eye
Audubon self-immortalizes. Opening
his enormous beak, he is
the American White Pelican
which holds forever forth

his lordly catch,
swallowing it all.

Donna Langevin

In the Café du Monde

jam packed
under the canopy seven days a week
you can order *beignets*
like puffy golden clouds
fried in a vat bigger than a bathtub.
Misted with icing sugar, they'll lift
your mood sky-high
as you sip café au lait
flavoured with roasted chicory
the colour of the Mississippi
from a "navy" mug.

Your eyes big as dinner plates,
you can watch a dozen shows
from your dirty street-side table —
boys tap-dancing with bottle caps nailed to their shoes,
a clown twisting balloons into a sausage dog,
Dante the magician in his stingy-brim Stetson
snatching a twenty-dollar bill out of an orange
while you sway in synch with a band
brassing up "the Saints" as the spirit
of Louis Armstrong parades in the air.

In the Café du Monde barely cooled
by fans whining like mosquitoes
you can share a table with
tourists lawyers gangsters
housewives gamblers merchants
ghosts of coffee bean farmers
exhausted from the French Market,
dropping in for a cup since 1862.

In the Café du Monde like the hub
of a captain's wheel
you can hear the voices of ships
on their way to Baton Rouge and Natchez,
Memphis and St. Louis.

You can meet a friend and wish
you could talk forever.
You can drink alone, yet pulse
with the heart of the world
as people come and go,
and past and present flow
from a brimming mug
into your own river-veins.

If "Live Oaks" Could Laugh

I would hear them all over New Orleans —
deep earthy rumblings rising from their roots
which reach back long before Bienville
scouted the swamp for a site.

I would float on waves spilling from ho-ho mouths
hidden behind their hoary beards
dripping diamond-rain.

And surely, I would weep with them
when laughter turned to grief as they mourned
for their limbs torn out by Katrina.

But when I heard a rude *slurp slurp*
sloshing through my sleep,
it would be that liquid joy welling up
their trunks as they guzzled
flood-water to replenish blood they lost.

Six months later at Mardi Gras
when the buds returned with élan
and shook out tiny parachutes
with green and golden strings,
the "Chocolate Oaks" — nicknamed after the flood —
would ladle a laugh as creamy and rich
as the mud on their bark.

Irrepressible as the people
who climb them to watch the parades,
they'd bow to fellow kings of merriment —
Bacchus, Zulu and *Rex* as beads tossed
from watermarked floats land in leafy canopies,
dazzle their new green crowns.

Ruth Latta

"Poetry Café" at a Retirement Residence

I braced myself for sentimental verse,
for doggerel at "Poetry Café",
some Kipling, Service, Tennyson and worse,
long narratives to fill me with dismay.

Yet it was heartening to see a crowd
to celebrate the love of craft and word —
a favourite childhood poem shared aloud
or classics loved for years and finally heard.

One senior lady read of "love more strong"
in old age, with its "glowing inner fire."
A man with fading eyes read Milton's song
about his blindness. Oh, how they inspire!

What wisdom and what insight they have shown
as they affirm the value of a poem!

Beth Learn

Bethie at the Beach

"The answer to which is, both of."

The forest was broadly familiar
Myriad old sadness and the superfluidity of stone
Long serene horizontal lines of more most morbid blue —
all the elements of despair
before which stand so absolutely still .....

I remember the sense that something must be done. Everything is at first confused and apparently in motion. The same way as the nail on which to hang verily as if behind in the past. The low silvery drift-where-it-would of sun-warmed tombs and extravagant flowers.

And on and on into the great dim rather rickety sheds and loose paraphernalia I sighed, I wandered, I walked up and down and in and out and whenever I could: The immense, the monstrous,   absolutely and exactly
I ADORE YOU COMPLETELY   (Poor dear me).
This, that having passed out of sight.   I knew so well what he meant.

And when as often happens in the first months of the war: Whether the world is real such as I now see it to have been at the time I lived through it. There is no other world possible in the sense in which mine is   M O R E   T H A N   M E   and that still wouldn't be enough. Little indeed living at all might have seemed and all so absurdly the scarcely less simplified green.

And suddenly, as from however now on the magic of the manner in which the mere looming mass of the more immeasurably much I mean or when having so little baked beautifully and hard.

The sustained fury of perception; as to something happy that we have irretreivably missed. The presence of a past in the sense of pre-exact. The true type of the monstrous seemed to be reached. Once in an unchanged world at the end of time....

That the sky all the same came down on him —
he couldn't keep it up.

Then the night past   (He didn't get through it)   "Goodbye, my dear!"
How we should otherwise have known him.

How can everything so have gone.   (What was it to get away.)   How could he ever as when he could be both rare and precise about the dreadful / is so essentially a thing to take or leave.   That, for which we may propose to approach at all intimately; its having to be not easily   some possible picture.

So one saw it: The bright hard sky.   The large firm nail driven in.   The almost uncanny inconsequence with which one —   YES!   With the finger.

The winter is bare and brown enough.
The sky in all directions dark

And then once more the tale was taken up: What it is that remains — the wake which it leaves. The considerable mass of what is NOT purely logical. Always in order for us to feel yet again: What it is we are held by.

I make the most of the ground already broken. The loud appeal not to be left out.
For what all the while and in which can it be mistakenly taken that but for this: How perfectly little one looked it well in the face. The real in the name of the possible quickening up.

One day all that is hoped for will have to make itself shown. Most of the many cruel bright stars. We, none of us have everything all to ourselves, that I was to remember.   There at which unfrightened distance there was still such a hole.   What Darwin means is:

The horror of difficulty — to remain in the dark. HERE LAY THE FEROCIOUS
Where can we be said to know (and if we knew that . . .

Love lifts us up.
Darksomely like the deep
a lingering earlier world in which
nothing had been
something richer and more relieved
by reason of them

A few things fail to fit: My Mother's gloves, my Grandmother's ring, terms into which I saw the real clamoring to be rendered. What shall I say in the way of the ponderously particular? The perpetual predicament of continuity. As many as possible of the little

holes in which they / those things in the dark either false or illicitly interpolated.
It was not by knowing them that she loved

Elsewhere, again and again. Repeatedly back into the sense of other years. The warm wave of the near and familiar. Things we cannot know "sooner or later". The blessed cause of occasional silence.   Our finally fatal sense....

Probably she will never come much closer to the truth. The long gasp vague when the individual swept through it says ever so elegantly,   *"Suppose there were no such reality"*. And you see now how we not only fail to remember.

If there is no more of it than this: Sufficiently large tastes of terrible incompleteness, things startled by the light, women silently weeping   "YOU LITTLE BASTARD!" and he wasn't coming back

Yet, something was always true. Neither of which is either ruled out.
I hold — I have.   You'll see soon enough. To make this which so deeply ought to be: *rough and ready.*

As the one condition of our being said to know it will as such at least be more than is revealed. How grimly the world (for the most part) waits to be less ugly again.

So I can sing as much as I will. If you feel fire at all ....
Truth, with no one thinking it.
Or, whether, if it have any . . .   What we need lose.

The real truth is a call across the water

The rise and drop again of the wave

To which we may lend

something of the light.

For my father, Glennis Eugene Learn, Sr., whose love for all things science inspired my ongoing art/science work in the Alice Springs Project

John B. Lee

Bringing the Farmhouse Down

I remember
being in the old
three-story blond brick
Middlesex county century farm home
breaking the ribs of the house
sledging lath
the horsehair plaster
with continental maps papered
and falling away
from the walls
of the vacant room
I was a small boy
barely able to lift
the head of the hammer
pulling strong nails
with a crowbar
easing them out
the ghost dust of a gritty trowel
unbuilding inward
from the peen-bruise of the punched studs
and the dry-lime fragrance
of the splintering slats
breathing in white-tongued dust
all day tasting the mined earth
what born-in-bed generations
were billowing to the knee
our hands powder-white
roughened by work
and nicked red through dirt
like the scoring of errors
my palms
bubbled with blebs
that I dare not break

in the long hall
the wicker wheelchair
winced like a toy
while the girls played
broken-legged doll

and the sun measured
morning with a brilliant melt
like tall butter
until in the long-shadowed
wane of bent darkness
we set
what leans
against what remained
and walked to the ankles
in the wrecked world
our shoes going *grief grief*
in the sorrow shuffle
of a disorganized result

and we washed away
the milk swirl
of our labour
found our faces
under rinsed masks
setting the soap cakes
down smaller for that
in the decorative lave cradle
of the sink

"you were a strange boy"
my aunt
says of me now
as I'd said to her
at supper
"well, we'll never have
that day again . . ."
as a world-weary
nine-year-old it seems I knew
even then
there was a glass
I emptied
and one I filled
both from the same deep well
the drained glass always
heavy with a second thirst

The Ungoable

it was the opposite of falling —
seeing her mother
waving from the shore
as she and her sisters
stood at the railing
of the ship
leaving Europe
after the war
her mother dimming
to a sorrowful deflation
a reified vanishment of love breaking the heart
the way the crag of a cove
breaks a wave
at the thin edge of the sea
one high sharp
exhilarating shatter-glass
moment of roaring
and sumping the rock hollows
to feel that unswallowable grief
the herniated ache
at the hiatus of an inheld sob
surely only a child
can hurt that way
yet I see
in the telling
how this lovely woman
relives the deep throb of loss
revivifying for the fräulein she was
born in Berlin
before the conflagration of the city
with its fire dead
immolated in the burning strausses
the Führer sneering
through flame flowers
rising from the red garlands of his bones

the Swastika
blasted by sappers
crashing to the earth

lightning in the high branches
and the eagle kinder
of the Phoenix with no future

she mentions
a certain officer of the conquering Soviet
lusting after her mother
who was beautiful
and when her mother refused
his unwanted advances
he lined up her five children
placed a loaded pistol to each
of their temples
touching the muzzle
to the pulse point of each young mind
that black zero's cold metallic kiss
and then firing a single shot
in the air at the end, so she knew
the inescapable consequence
of a mother's refusal

and the same dignified
and much-loved mother
violated by the cruelty
of a choice
that is no choice

stood on the pier at the shore of the harbour
waving
her hand like the last glimpse
of the desperate drowned

those who are helpless in history
because they know by the needle of some inner compass
the ungoable direction of hope

On kindness

write the word *love* on one side
of a single sheet
of white bonded paper
and then
write the word *hate*
on a second
let each leaf drift loose
from the same height
at exactly the same moment
keeping in mind
the scholar's parable of a pound
of feathers
and even given the drop-weight of heavy words
you notice a sameness
as they
fall through the invisible calipers of time
all the while wondering
at the value of loft
and the measure of ink
knowing how the wet wing
tips in flight to almost touch the rising wave
or the shadow
spreads in the brilliant gloom
of its own reflected worth
subsiding to soft grey in a second light
with a different source
or as it is
with the lucent green
of filmy water gulping a plunging stone
disappearing beneath the echo-rhythms of a radiant O

think here
of the human heart
how it daps on the wrist then vanishes
like a pinch in silk

say your father
enters the story
and you are a boy
at his table
having trimmed the fat
and left it
oiling the plate
at the close of the meal
and there it lay
in white refusal
a greasy remnant of your appetite
and he says

"you shall not leave this table
until you have finished
every scrap"

and you lay your fork aside
cross your arms
and concentrate
on the cut lines
in the gristle
and the marbling of slivered meat
meanwhile the shine congeals
as it cools and scums the surface
and you wonder why he insists

you know you will not comply
you will stay forever if need be
what do you care
for love or hate

say then
your grandfather enters the story
on a different day
he places his hand on your wrist
catching his breath
as you climb together what for him
is a difficult hill
and you want your father to know
how slowly you walked
how full of care
how light his hand like a breeze in the hair
how laboured his breathing
how heavy his old heart a stone beating in the breast
like the sorrowful drumming of black cloth

and the words land light
and the words land hard

and love lifts as it falls
and hate falls as it lifts
and the two together
play like the mating of gulls

and you are still at the table
and you remain forever
half-way up the hill
with the hand-weight of a ghost
you must carry
as a great tree carries the shade

Bernice Lever

Young Eyes Ask Why

Young eyes ask why
as puzzling behind
thick lenses
of gas masks
as they try to see
our reasons,

Even our reason:
which we lost as we swam
neck-deep in
our own sewage
searching for that button
for that last glorious fling
at world destruction.

Don't question, children;
just erase any trace
of humanity,
just corrode and corrupt
all you touch.

Do as we do.

shinny Hockney - *David Haskins*

Norma West Linder

Little Boy Lost

It's difficult to write
about a child
who, according to
the newspaper account,
begged to go back
to his mother in Jamaica
who wanted him
to have a better life
in Canada.

The words
keep getting
soaked with blood
keep slipping
through the cracks.

A quiet little boy
the neighbors said
— a little boy
who didn't go
to school.

After his stepmother's
final beating
the pathologist
found a tooth
in his stomach.

Last Poem for Irving Layton

>*They are not long, the days of wine and roses*
>*Out of a misty dream*
>*Our path emerges for awhile, then closes*
>*Within a dream*
>   - Ernest Dowson, 1867-1900

A quiet woman, never far from tears
I contemplate the irony of life
how it often ends
not as we wish
but in implacable disintegration
They are not long, the days of wine and roses

You wanted pitchforks blazing as you left
striding with manly rage into the void
Instead, your memory failed; your daily smoke
was all that you had left of fire that burned
with such intensity
Out of a misty dream

I conjure you, and I sincerely wish
your slow departure into the unknown
your entry through that door marked Nevermore
could have been the one that you desired
Our path emerges for awhile, then closes
Within a dream

Annick MacAskill

Tatiana in Gaspra, 1902
    after a photo by Sophia Tolstoy

Father's flesh has faded from his bones —
his second-to-last rites your last blessings
in the duchess's Crimean cottage,
where sunlight bleaches out his lips, the romance
of his hands curved
about a desk, a notebook; under the stink of camphor,
the milky gaze and the refusal that have endured
his years and yours — canvases and suitors
the bewilderment of his ongoing.

There is no meeting without body:

his spine a greased chain
under onion skin, a wool coat,
pupils blazing towards the adoration
eight years down the road. Gratitude
is now imperative: remind yourself
that daughters don't do anything for glory,
and pray.

Carol Malyon

the morgue attendant & his wife

vases clutter the kitchen cupboard
baskets stacked in a hall closet
fall over whenever the door is opened

delivered by hearse
to the hospital back door   funeral baskets
so obvious where they came from

he brings them home   why not?   patients
don't want reminders of a final destination

roses are her favourite   a breath of summer
& iris   symbol of spring

he hurries to get home first
rearranges them on the hall table
so she'll see them when she comes in the door

he hurries to shower   scrub   shampoo
lest the formaldehyde stink still lingers

click   a key in the lock

carnations!   she reaches out to touch them
arranging her face   knowing he watches
from the shadows   waits to be touched next

they clutch   insistent   skip supper   tumble into bed

'quick' he says before he thinks
quick   that biblical word   meaning alive
the opposite of dead

he closes his eyes   she always teases
thinks it's sweet   'you're too beautiful'
he tells her   'i can't bear to look'

her pale body sprawled beneath him
stretched out on a cool white sheet

he inhales her cologne   his fingers tangle her hair
his fingerprints are all over her body
as he whispers against her ear
'you're so warm   so warm   so warm'

Blaine Marchand

In the White Giant's Thigh

Determined, the nurse draws the white coat
about her, the way I clasped my nightdress
that morning as dawn bled into the waters
trickling along the folds of the estuary.

So calculating, the doctor's needle slides
under the skin, effortlessly as Dylan
when a woman lies soft as sand beneath him.

How I hate what he has made me. He who writes:
"O Caitlin, my love, my Cat, my lovely love",
then spends his drunken self pummelling some bitch.

Legs up, feet in the stirrups, it's almost
if lying here I am giving myself to him.
But the doctor is not here for that reason.

"Was it a girl? Was it a girl?" I want to know.
He ignores me, just like a man goes about his work,
diligently as Dylan dissecting emotion and thought,
stitching lines and rhymes with the thread of voice.

His hands run red as he hacks at the foetus.
It comes out bit by bit. Only three months to term.
But I want to go to America too. I am not
a moral coward. I want just a bit of fun.

My feet are cold as that morning I crept
out on the sands at low tide searching
for fragments of his poem. The night before,
angry and jealous at its unmitigated conceit,
my hatred found scissors, slashed
at that creation of his. My hands tore
through an opening in the window, hurled
the work piecemeal into the dead of night.

The next morning I cradled the shreds, placed them
on the kitchen table as a token. He looked away,
cowed by the vengeance of shifting tide. Mutely
he swept them into his small white palm and withdrew.

Life is a Train

Each of us must stand in line,
wait for this journey to begin.
The scurry of hundreds of leather soles,
the thud of reggae music from a kiosk
against the concrete walls of la gare centrale,
irritate this random queue of bone-weary
business people, shoppers thrown together
simply because it is time to depart.

In the narrow tunnel below ground each of us settles
down into the confines of our seat.
A British boy faces me in camouflage pants and cap,
an ill-fitting man's tweed coat,
runs his fingers over and over the dust jacket
of Dostoevsky's *The House of the Dead*.
A schoolgirl, beside me, in uniform, conjugates,
again and again, the passé composé of the irregular verb vivre.
I rummage through my briefcase, retrieve
the selected poems of Delmore Schwartz.

Randy, the last time we spoke we argued about Schwartz.
Such a complex man. The promise of acclaim;
the fears that held him, consumed him:
sexuality, anti-Semitism, rejection.
I found him insufferable; you, more than the sum of his parts.
I thought of your mind, like phosphorescence,
trapped in a body that had not
properly worked since you were born.
I always remember you at nineteen
passionate about the writings of Gide and Genet,
your laughter raucous at life's absurdity,
and then the quiet despair.
Once again your summer would be spent
in the hospital, just as you had every year of your life.

Now twenty years later, the fight it took
just to keep going is over.
Your body finally has had its way.
I didn't even know you had been hospitalized;
never had the chance to say good-bye,
to tie everything neatly up as if it were a poem.
I flip open the book, Schwartz's words leap out at me:
"How the false truths of the years of youth have passed!
Have passed at full speed like a train which never stopped."

Zakat

Beyond the roses, which detonate from earth in explosive
crimson, the mosque is illuminated by morning light.

Blue and white tiles incandescent, a flourish of lilies against which
the faithful move — women in white burqas like doves,

men in hand-woven shawls encumbering shoulders.
These believers stroll, step out and beyond the shadows

condensed on the ground, dark residue left by gunpowder.
Their lips still flavoured by suhoor, bodies not yet craving

nourishment but braced for cleansing, their hearts
divining purity from worldly activities, inner souls freed

from harm. At one corner, a young boy in a wheelchair,
his legs scarred stumps, extends a hand for zakat.

I conjure the pressure of his soles that day he walked
across a field — perhaps lagging behind playmates

or tending to goats — while from below its surface
the trap sparked forth, entangling him in its fierce release

of metal and energy, shattering him in a split second
of confusion, blood and pain. He smiles at me,

his palm opening, as if in prayer, an aperture for the coins
that now burden my pockets. Exposed to the sunlight

they have the effervescence of fireworks igniting the sky.
As I release them, they are the plumage of the birds

the seller in the courtyard has bartered into the hands
of pilgrims. With these offerings we all are released

from the heat and pain of this charred earth,
our voices, like wings, vibrate in the air, repentant with chant.

Song of Little Squirrel

"Before the white people came, we did what we wanted. When our hearts said move, we did. When our mouths cracked with thirst and the land lolled under the heat like a tongue, we went with our gourds to where there was water. When our stomachs thundered with hunger, our men read hooves pressed into the earth and hunted the animals as they moved to other grasslands.

"When the white people first came to this place, I was already a young woman with breasts. I was called Little Squirrel. Our people said this woman's face shall never know ugliness. Even my sister said give me your face for mine is too long. Together we sang of my beauty.

"Once my people lived across this vast plain. To visit took many days. When villagers met, a great feast took place. Voices joined the wind in the trees. Food was plentiful. We shared.

"Now the white people who rule from afar say: stay in this place. We have set it aside for you. We will take care of you. We will bring you food. But there are too many people and not enough food. They give us mealie meal. Our stomachs rumble with pain each time we eat it. People are dying of TB. When I was a young girl, we moved and left sickness behind. I have five children. My TB tag gets extra meal for them.

"But I am woman of means. I make money from tourists. I dress myself like my mother when she was my age. People stop and take pictures. This money does not buy my happiness. The villagers accuse me of hoarding things, of not sharing my wealth. I call them liars. I say I have nothing to hide. Everything I have you can see — my children's blankets, my husband's and my clothes. They say I drink beer while they starve. Buy us food. Buy us shoes. I tell them we must not bicker, we are one people, we must be strong. They tell me I insult them, that I lie.

"A preacher comes to talk of his Jesus. I go to listen and laugh. Who is this man who calls himself the son of God? Why would God choose to suffer? He must be crazy. We don't believe such a thing. The army comes into our area. We call them owners of death. They think we look up to them but we just smile. They play their games. Even when they joke they are like warriors. They steal our young with words of a better life, of money, of food. Our young men are happy. We watch our sons being taken away like cattle in trucks. Sorrow silences us.

"When I was a young woman I was called Little Squirrel. People said this woman's face shall never know ugliness. Now the villagers scorn me, abuse me. Death mocks me, dances with me. I cry don't look at my face."

NOTE: *Written after viewing the film* N`Ai, Story of a Kung Woman

Steven McCabe

Lament of A Fool in the Tradition of Sacrifice, Folly, and Clairvoyance

Bang! Bang! Bang!
Soldiers and frontiersmen shoot into the warm olive groves from passing
Trains. Imagine the sound.
Bulldozers pile branches, triumphantly staging tintype photographs.

I blow into a bone whistle:
Resonant echoes compete with the seen and unseen machinery.

Marksmen yank open creaking & jammed windows,
Cinders & sparks brush their faces, their blinking eyes take aim,
Winchester repeating rifles blast away unloading gale-force flashes of heat and lead,
Moist wooden circles take shots to the heart —
Quivering circles at zero point.
Branch-arms cradle the memory of vast grasslands,
Vibrations of buffalo hooves curve slightly ever upwards into shaking branches,
Olives fall like unseeing eyes.

I wear the green of Green Man, the green of Green George, shaking the bells
Adorning my coxcomb hat,
Alerting stationary groves & the great herds of shaggy beasts.

A bulldozer creaks and shudders lifting metal buckets filled with teeth and lips,
I sing into the din:
Why does the morning bird sing after dark?
If your bed is made of fire, may you be fireproof.
Love is the spoon that lifts the water.
I lift my voice against rain that is no rain.

I pinch my lips & mimic the low rumble of grazing herds,
Reverberate into roots, reaching into the underground
Where birth regenerates the seasonal cycle orbiting the sun.
Gnarly forearms erupt into leaf and fruit.
I divine the weather &
Clap my hands above baskets filled with shadows.

I try to confuse the driver by spinning counter-clockwise
Sounding whistles and clicks interspersed with high-pitched caws.
I stir unseen, enormous cauldrons,
Funnel pebbles into rifle barrels,
Slam windows shut,
Press buttons and yank levers,
Attempt to deflate studded, rubber wheels hard as magma, large as boulders
Bullets pass through me cracking the horn of my spine.
I juke between stampeding legs, hang onto a tail, dragged & dragged & dragged!
Sleep with my master's hounds where I do not wake.

The noonday sun warming & ripens the fruit of the tree,
Woozy newborns balance & strengthen their legs.

Resonant echoes haunt the unseen machinery
Lingering in the air like bells shaking & shaking & shaking!

Elizabeth McCallister

Noticing the Scenery

I watch the scene.
Checking it out.
I catch a man's eyes.
Assess the situation.
Experts say this is normal:
you can't help but notice the scenery

Travelling alone
airlines will assign me
a seat between two men.
Flights seem shorter when
I practice my flirting
making conversation with strangers.

One man asks me how I
have such blue eyes.
So I wonder if I could pick him up,
or is he just practising too?

When I feel guilty,
(not often enough)
I remember I'm supposed to be
a chaste woman.
Not only spoken for
but taken.

Mori McCrae

Gravity

I lie awake, inert beneath blankets
the hand of mild, winter depression
holds me to the pillow
as my husband takes his readings.

In the early morning light, he sits, arm embalmed
before a small machine. I listen as it hums and shunts,
observe the dollop of flesh that hangs from his elbow
like a ball on the rung of an abacus.

The readings are low — too low:

$$\frac{111}{68} \qquad \frac{114}{71} \qquad \frac{122}{78}$$

"That's a good one —"
jotting down the number
he releases his arm
chops another pill in half
and heads out into
the porcelain-cold morning
an arabesque of snow replacing him,
leaves a puddle by the door.

Ian McCulloch

Poppa

I knew the story of how
at seventeen, fighting in France
a shell burst wrenched the ground over him,
killed the rest of his gun crew
and held him suffocating in its tight fist,
buried with the bodies of his comrades
open mouths wedged with the abrupt sediment
of their truncated lives,
the racket of their sudden end.

I was pale and timid in his presence.
He was perpetually beyond the reach
of my immature voice,
his face brown and bristled
seemed somehow closed
as I watched him put away
the round shell of the earplug
with the white whistling box
from his shirt pocket.
Sound sleeping somewhere else for him

I expected to see sand pouring
onto the bedroom floor
from the barren canals of his vacant ears.
Afraid of the dark in that old house,
lying next to him in his bed
my ear against his.
I trembled thinking of him
under the ruined, ruptured earth,
pinned against his dead companions,
intimate under that dense blanket,
the viscous silence convulsing in his skull.

I listened for some echo of the concussion
that had pressed him, still only a boy,
into a premature and crowded grave.
Never considering until now
how this must change someone,
twist something deep or how
so much was spoiled all those years
before we would know each other.
The dark from that
black sulphur-choked hole
seeping into my days
with a longing for lost light
and the transitory static that would become
our only spoken love.

Infirmity and old age whittled him down
before I figured out some way to unearth
an open line of communication.
My last memory of him
is my mother telling the story
of how he smacked an orderly
and stood defiantly on the bed.
Back off you sonavubitch, he bellowed
swinging the colostomy bag
in long yellow arcs over his head.
Ready for all comers,
keeping everyone at bay.

Inconsolable and wild
beyond the reach of persuasion.
Like a soldier making his last stand
or a swimmer going down
for the third time.
Like someone who knew
the bitter dimensions of death.

Carl Martin's Tongue Stuck To The Merry-Go-Round

Tubular metal
red paint flaking
from the bent
pipe shapes
the wooden seats
rough and cold
barely clearing
a snow-packed landscape
the school yard frenetic
with recess and
Carl a bored cog
in the engine
that turned us
licked a steel curve
and found himself stuck
to a burning imperative
circling gracelessly
behind his stretched tongue
and when the bell rang
we all deserted him

after all
any attempts at a solution
would only make us late
and the clanging duty
echoing across
the frigid morning
asked only for a
rank and file presence
so with tongues still
safely tucked in our heads
we could only leave him
stumbling alone
on the spoked wheel
of our obligation
to the iron creaking
of our frozen laughter
trampling his own footsteps
over and over again

when they found him
minutes later and
came with warm water
to ease his flesh
from its crystalline attraction
he was still pushing
the empty merry-go-round
either chasing a resolution
he hadn't the courage
to face or running
from the cold taste
of his vowelless predicament
he couldn't escape
the parable because
he searched the same
circular direction
remaining faithful
to protocol
already fluent
in his own
small mute pain

Susan McMaster

Sign of Respect

Afraid she's fallen or had a stroke
when she doesn't answer my knock,
I have the nurse unlock her door,
ignoring with a daughter's disdain
the clearly written note —
"Do Not Disturb"
in her school teacher hand —
stuck above the knob —

And can only laugh,
with surprise and a kind of
relief and delight,
to see two bare bodies
half rise on the bed
as I step in.

"Sorry! — " I back out fast.

Who gave me the right
to breach a shut door?

What made me sure
age had smothered that flame?

> *I may be losing my memory, but it's a discriminating memory. I have things you will never know — no matter what I remember or forget. There are places in my mind where you can never go.*

How God sees

Look out from top
of the Gatineau Hills,
lean over the stone wall
at the Parkway's edge,
and cover the whole expanse
of glittering green
in one wide sweep,
know, without tracking it,
how the river bends,
twists through fields
that lie like pillows
on their limestone bed,
how roads stitch between.

One glance, it's all there.

And then, pick a leaf
from the ivy on the wall,
cup it in your fingers,
trace the fine veins,
bend closer,
see —

The whole wide valley
focus in a green beam
along a slender rib —

ray out to the rim.

Bronwen McRae

At the A & W

I watch them from two tables over. Old men
performing the retirement ritual. Meet for coffee
at A & W. There are at least twelve of them. They talk quietly
and I name them, put words in their mouths.

Amil sits in the middle. It's his year to cheer.
He's all blue for the Leafs. They've made the playoffs
and Amil is all in. Cap, jersey,
even the jacket hung on the back of his chair.
This year they're gonna do it. I can't wait
forever. Don't know how many good years I got left.

Lou is on the end. He's got those chunky socks
and his pants are too short. He lifts his tweed hat,
scratches his brow. He's listening to Al prattle on,
and it's hard because he's heard this story before.
That, and it's just getting harder to concentrate these days.

Al lost his wife six months ago. He knows he's driving the guys
crazy, but he just can't stop talking about it. *What kind of person refuses*
treatment? She wasn't too old to fight. She wasn't.
Lou hands him a handkerchief. Al grabs it and swipes at his face.

They have this standing engagement. Whoever can make it.
Every week since they retired from working the rails.
Clayton pipes up *You know which one they've abandoned now?*
Loreburn to Broderick. I worked that line for forty five years.
And Mossbank to Hodgeville? On the chopping block. My son told me.
Said he read it on . . . The Internet.

My coffee has gone cold so it's time to leave. I smile at these men
as I make my way to the exit. One old fellow
smiles back at me. His eyes are bright blue beneath the rail line wrinkles.
His wink seems to say *I saw you watching. I know you get it. Everyone*
has a story.

Going Back

He is more than his drunken father,
more than hungry
hip bones and thick foggy lenses.
His leg muscles strong, he walked away

from long days of train yard labour
coal smudged memories of a burly
backhand for a high school punk unable
to keep up.

Pictures himself back there
someday, ahead of the game,
sneering at a life that treated him
poorly.

But even as he thinks this, he knows
revenge doesn't come in a pretty package,
never shows up

in a crisp new suit.

icicle - *Henry Beissel*

Rhonda Melanson

Strong Women

i

play penny whistles and drums
       in Alaskan string bands
lilt their chords in clear Juneau air
wearing calico frocks and red stilettos.
They laugh at my naiveté.

ii

Tracy Arm chunks her boxes of cool
             into chilled fjord.
They are deep, blue tonics
I want to drink hastily before they
evaporate from the cracked glass
that I bring to her last call.

iii

I now face the Palestinian women
         in auctioned paintings
adorned in crimson and bold strokes
who later bare their bushes
wiry scribbles against creamy flesh.
I yearn for their brazen nakedness
their pride in plump, milky thighs
            and lumpy raw breasts.

But my eyes cannot go there
I am only Delilah, cutter of hair

One Catholic's Apology for Residential Schools

Years ago we wrote a book
called *The Indian In The Box*

We unhinged
those black boards

till they screeched like chalk
with dust settling as white guilt.

Our narrated version
on straight-laced lines

sullied by those times
the red pen exploded

blood
whose liquid memory drips.

We still pretend they are stigmatas
borne of our righteousness

rather than penance
for our red and white shame

our need to pray
for bleached grace from the sun

appease our Creator.

Bruce Meyer

My Father's Passing Contained No Poetry

i)

The rhythm of monitored hearts
and jagged lines struck like lightning
in cold, fluorescent, arterial halls
left me wondering if too long a life
had broken his heart in so many places.

On days when he sat up
to answer yes, or no, or not at all,
his food stank of its former selves,
yet he swallowed it the way one swallows fate
because he needed to say he had fought his end.

And the frosted windows were of no use.
They kept the world bottled up inside him
the way paradise is locked away in thoughts
or moments torn from a long, hard night;

and I wanted to remind him
of days when we must have known it,
a Cape wind scented with raindrop pine
mixed by the strong arm of salt air.

I wanted to sing old songs with him
and set him adrift among beautiful dreamers,
but the man in the next bed hit the floor,
and we both forgot the lyrics we knew
and how they melted like November snow
or a conversation we couldn't continue.

ii)

Last summer in New York I rode a bus
from Tryon Park in north Manhattan
down Broadway in a greasy traffic jam,
the cogs grinding in the city's machine
waiting to burst into windows of starlight,
a million points in digital frames,
each one signalling that life goes on;   >>>

and the bus settled in the heat for an hour
among aging apartments in Washington Heights
until the street's slope prevailed
and we slid southward to the shores of Columbia
where he spent his summers among giants of thought —

Hayakawa, Du Bois, and Buckminster Fuller,
the geodesic domes of futures to come
trying to shape tomorrows around ideas,
and I wondered what would have become of him
had life's practicalities not seized his soul.

I see him standing knee-deep in dreams
sparkling like fragments of shattered glass
a shop keeper sweeps on the streets of Harlem
because one broken window leads to the next.

iii)

I'd give anything now to ask you questions,
but the last line you ever rode
straight as Broadway until it veered,
was a flat line disappearing in a maze
bound to be bent, made to be broken,
perhaps poetic, though a straight-shooter's quest:

and I try in my thoughts to add New York's ways,
the calculation of avenues and streets,
waiting for the sum I can never conclude;
and being the son who was bad at math

I have nothing to offer except this gift:
it is merely poetry.
It serves no purpose.
It arrives uncomely as a hospital trolley.
It is footsteps down a cadeusial hall
where shadows robed in hospital gowns,
seek what it lost in losing life;

and taking my arm for your final walk
remark quietly, as if not breathing,
they could use some artwork on these walls.

The Death of Christianity in Oil City
for James Deahl

*". . . and there shall be no more death,
neither sorrow, nor crying . . ."*

Because spent oil seeks out its maker
and flows like a river to wash away sin,
it pulses beneath the iron bridge
and runs unknown as unknown names
behind the Woodlawn Cemetery Gates.

Because the dead are embraced by stone
and laid beneath tablets of palimpsest names
in scars of strip mines and hill stigmata,
the living recall their battle for heaven,
and the fallen their earth beyond Sambation.

Because the earth is rusted as prayers
and curses are surnames of everlasting life,
churches are boarded with crucifixion nails,
and those who believe live abandoned to faith,
on side street outcrops mapped by desire,
and desire extinguished in the rage to believe.

If rage becomes the will of faith
carved lengthwise through these Allegheny hills
it bears the image of a maker's best work,
hills rolling like waves at mid-sea,
churches battened like temple doors,
and the temple fallen to the broken heart.

Because the heart drilled hard through shale,
and shale has bled to move the world,
there is no oil for the tabernacle lamp,
and holy, holy, holy of all holies,
the past lies abandoned with all it took,
with a fire that purifies the world from sin.

>>>

The fire that purifies the world from sin
lived in the daylight behind iron clouds,
shone as a beacon down a valley's deep breath,
tarnished and polished by the path it took,
a beacon whose name once looked unto hills
with a love that endured in the heart of Oil City,
and flowed like a river that runs through the world,
a place to name the flesh of man,
a place to begin the life of the soul,
as it flowed through time to redeem mankind,
and coursed to a realm where there is no death.

The place that is said to be free of death
can only be reached through the fire of pain,
lives that ached like a river with wings,
yet could not fly to the heaven they saw
and drilled through rock to steal its fire,
held as secrets in pages of shale,
because spent oil seeks out its maker,
and burns as a river reborn at the sea.

To believe was to say the dead could travel.
To believe was to say they could reach the sea.
The churches are ships turned upside down.
They rot on beachheads, their ratlines are limp.
Their painted prow eyes see no more.
In the depths of the earth there is no more sea.

Two Students on the College Lawn

Leaving my office late after teaching
a night class on love poetry's spell,
I find two students woven on the grass,
their bodies pale as textbooks beneath stars.
They are studying each other's eyes,
exchanging words of wordless tongues
moving to touch a beauty without sound.
It is a night where poetry is whispered,
the air as if a conspiracy of breath,
or a sigh of summer learning to survive
the outset of another term. I pass them
the way a shadow floats upon a wall
when everything is breathless, a night
when lovers learn what love is before
love cheats them of its mystery, a time
to feel the softness of another's skin
and the rhythm of breath against the world.
I envy them, lying there, silent and starry,
their futures locked inside their souls
as each eye reads the other's eyes
to see if ghosts of future knowledge
haunt them as they haunt each other.
Tomorrow, they will recall tonight
as the time they made poetry out of life
and spoke by heart until the heart stood still.

Michael Mirolla

To a poet struggling to recover her words

Please note: this is not a metaphor.

In the spongy grey room, walls reticulated,
bony chair bolted to upheaving floor,
spotlight at 10 flickers per minute,
she sits. There's a hole in the side
of her head. There's a hole where they
extracted the over-eager building blocks,
the out-of-control tidbits of DNA.
The incisions were precise, one must assume.
But it didn't prevent the words . . . her words . . .
from escaping into the sterile air.

Now, a saintly smile framing her face,
she sits in the bony chair inside
the spongy grey room with reticulated walls
and reaches out to recapture
the stray letters that may or may not
have survived without her tender care.

I sit across from her, spoon-feeding
alphabet strands into a hungry mouth
fearful that the words that have kept her whole
that have defined her
that connect her to herself
that have built this grey room
will be unable to make the return journey.

Please note: This has not been a metaphor.

The Bear

When you hear the sound of scraping beyond
a cave's orifice to the outer world
think again before you enter. The warmth
the smell the heady brew may invite you
into a place of origin a place
where fermentation lacks but your quick yeast.

Inside you may find luminescent walls
covered with the true signs of art: clasp square
dove vase. And the word: *Rückgeburt*. Rebirth.
Millennia accordioned into a single moment.
From the rutted plateaus of Anatolia
to the quickbog zones of the boreal north.

Or you may find the creature squatting
in the goddess pose as agonized she
prepares to insert a careless child back
into her womb. And are you next in line?
One more sacrifice to help atone for
that original chromosomal split?

Best to hold back until the scraping ends
the walls pristine the odors turned to must
the cave abandoned to bats and their echoes.
And then to gingerly step in with lantern
in hand to light the intimate corners
where androgyny failed to stop the great divide.

The bones gathered in ceremonial piles
wait for their owners to claim them. Totems
for the journey that lies ahead. A way
out of the maze that threatens to undo
us all. Gather those marked for you. Prepare
to carry them to where they no longer matter.

Lynda Monahan

taken away

through jackpine and tamarack
you climb the root knotted trail
to the head of the rapids
where you wade deep
push off and out
into the Churchill's foam and crash

the river owns you now

sealsleek you ride the dark center
through this howling white wound of water
beneath you gigantic heads of boulders
grazing your toe tips
as you are thundered along
the constant going under

your whole self just taken away

then sudden as that
you reach the eddy downstream
where you kick   kick hard
toward the cat tails at the water's edge
heave yourself up on the stonecobbled shore
your heart's current dancing
to the way the water wants you

ready to give yourself
to this river   all over again

A.F. Moritz

Baltimore May 2015

Baltimore oriole singing from the tip
of a vast, spreading silver maple, and then
he goes quiet and flies, "swift as arrow", deep
into neighbor trees — his gold and blue
hardly visible up under the dazzling
dull sky. Last week they were burning Baltimore,
the never solaced wound of the African
never let heal, chains and bullets, the angry
contentment of the others schooling themselves hard
in the delusion: then is then and now is now.
The rose-colored crab apples are almost done
with snowing: they're clouds mostly green,
though over there a hungry sparrow can knock
a flurry of pink out of one. But the white crab tree
still is fresh, dropping nothing, dense,
and opening inward — indescribable thought-like
ways of passage among petals
for the air it freshens. Behind it: the closed,
quiet house front: a face of supreme
beauty pondering, with a look, all outward,
that doesn't know or care how it looks. Under
the hedge, the gold forsythia flowers on the sidewalk
are skirts with empty central hollows awaiting
minuscule waists, a new human, girls
an inch tall, incorruptible, and somewhere already
dancing and laughing, naked, tasting each other's
lips, breasts, thighs, and the closed spaces
where frills and openings hide — the way
the wrinkled bark, the groins of limbs,
the passages to the interior of the tree,
all hide in the white petals. The way that the coming
race of humans, all female still in early embryo,
unthreatened, couples now,
beyond sight,
in a long lost scripture, not yet written,
in the orgy of imagination.

Philosopher and Southern Ohio

Praise those who finding themselves
alive on earth
pick up the work. Day after day
it never ends except that they call death
heavenly rest, and feel no guilt
in accepting it, as long as it comes late,
after a long or hard enough term of bearing
with the pain of the others. Only to die young
is a weakness, almost a sin — so fair
in a song it can make them cry. Praise them,
they hammer in a mine days and nights
and in the times remaining drive a mule
and an iron-prowed wood plough
on a steep slope for food. They help to poison
their own streams. They blame
themselves only, and jealously, joyfully
singing, they preserve the old way
of those who blame themselves. Their God
is innocence — he doesn't exist as I
would require him to and still he makes
the truth of the world be the dandelion
that the eyes fall on as a breeze starts
freshening summer, and the man towels his forehead . . .
the long road of dawn as he comes up
at shift's end . . . the people all together
for the dead friend at a hilltop churchyard
with shadows of the circling hawks
sweeping their feet . . . the ugly people
all saints, the community in one place
around the body . . . But no more rest.
The straggle of stores and cabins
under green ridges came, struggles
to maintain itself, later will be gone.
They never rest except for death
and they do not think the worry that spoils sleep
and the fear that twists dreams
are forecasts of the content of oblivion.

Names of Birds

Awake at dawn, recalling my father, crying,
unable to go to sleep again, and pretty soon
the first bird sings. Despair: when the first bird sings
and the first light comes and you haven't slept.
I curse myself: the many-noted melody
is its signature but I can't read its name.
My father knew the name of every bird,
every tree, bush and grass they played in,
every seed, bug and worm they ate. Their friend.
I've lived to an age far past what he received
and know nothing. Father, where are you
so I can ask you and have you give me
the names? I always thought I'd take the time,
later, to learn them from you. My father knew
the name of every bird. And I see now: he knew
not just the name of every kind but every one.
A scientist, he'd tell you birds have no names,
names are for people. But each bird does have a name,
a strange sort of word that exists only an instant
as it sings back to someone who greets it
and then it pauses, hoping to hear him again.

Deborah A. Morrison

Crystal Beach

Sunlight shines
on Crystal Beach, I feel the
peace of summer days.

Water calm, sand warm,
beautiful wings ascend upwards,
heart and soul fly free.

Barefoot walk at Crystal Beach,
clear lake is still, all is silent,
enchanted summer afternoon.

As I wander along the shore,
my heart knows peace,
my spirit does soar.

Sun on lake, shines like crystal,
serenity of summertime.

forest fingers - *Debbie Okun Hill*

Colin Morton

Last Rites

With the albums of snapshots
pretty as a postcard
go the half-spent rolls of wrapping paper,
old *Time* and *People* magazines,
half jars of relish,
the dried pens she meant to buy refills for,
and my mother's button jar
I used to sort — coloured and clear ones,
navy buttons with anchor insignia —
beach pebbles picked up on travels,
seashells in which you can hear the tide,
all the memories that once clung to these things
like coral to stone.
                    All go
since our own weigh heavy already
and we want to travel light when we go.
The snaps we once made fun of, these we keep,
if only to bury in closets of our own:
Mom in front of a mountain or cathedral
smiling with friends none of us knew
or knew she knew, on field trips we
were no part of, with X and Y,
without Z, who must have been behind the lens.

Furniture went first, to family or friends in town,
the Sally Ann, or just as far as the curb;
hazardous lamps with hanging heads and scruffy cords;
the toaster that either scorched or left the bread limp;
unreadable diskettes with copies of letters
we discarded soon after they arrived at our doors.
The walker and oxygen tanks go back to the clinic
where someone is breathlessly waiting.

Garbage bags of unsorted debris pile up at the door,
and someone has to rummage
for the coffee maker discarded in haste,
for now her apartment is bare
we can't just lock the door and go
the way she did, too suddenly.

So we stand, door open,
for last goodbyes, one more story.
We have been too hasty,
impatient to finish the unwanted job.
The coffee is stale, she long ago lost the taste for it.
But we linger at the kitchen counter,
nowhere left to sit,
and wonder which of us will be next
to impose this burden on the others.
A story that always made us laugh
has a hollow echo now.
We look into one another's eyes
a bit longer than usual, uncertain
who should take her keys and lock the door.

Marion Mutala

Seductress

She looks at me with magnetic dark eyes
One glance my way, one flash, it's over
One glimpse, one wink, she's mine
The temptress, destroyer, seductress
Sweat when I see her

Terrified she draws me into her embrace
My lady, lover, world
I smell her, lick my lips, enchanted by her perfume
Enticing
I am done

The glass reflects her image
Our poisonous relationship
My lady of night

She falls asleep in my arms
My bottle of lust, my sparkling bottle of rum
Slowly, one ounce at a time

Lois Nantais

A Prayer to the Wild

I picked a fight while you smiled
through your brain cancer
I'm not dead yet
You laced up your boots to amble the fields
Together and without a common faith
We walked, only with love straight through
To the reforested pines
This Eden, a bedstead of needles dry and dead
Speaking of life
Leaving us
About the day after the flood recedes
And you are gone
My uncle Noah
With no arc here to save the rest of us
There is only the mud

I am not dead yet
But our path leaves sores — blisters of the unsaid on our feet
As we pile our way through the brambles
Climb the escarpment to watch the sun set over the treeline
I will see you again
But how can you, uncle, with only bowed heads in your skies
If I kneel it is not for surrender, not to empty this garden
Of knowledge and fruit
There is no place for what has bloomed in me
This wild without the church of dogma
Informing the way
Yet, we are together on a path

I will see you again
Your last words to me
As we held to the possibility
Of a parting sea
And a quiet twig in the mouth of a dove

Shane Neilson

Angelic Salutation

1. Out of ether, halothane, and drugged-down
   brain-sate they gave me q.i.d — I rose to meet
   my mother in the afternoons. The ceiling
   in carousel blur and then her, a blue dress
   in a chair. The blent psychiatric air: I opened
   my eyes, and she was there. The ruminant
   hospital gave me to her, or her to me: knocked
   down in thought, shackled in act, she didn't care.
   She waited for me every inpatient day.
   She could leave. I had to stay.

2. Now she's infected and almost dead. In the ICU,
   bedridden, tubes enter her head two-by-two.
   Drains snake from her belly cut transverse
   and wide. What does she have inside? A *me* once
   long ago, but now internal burns from the purulent
   burst. I felt such stellated abuse in my nerves once
   when I wanted, but now I don't want the worst.
   I want her eyes to rise up and escape the drug-clenched
   arteries and opiates dousing an incredible fire.
   Watching the brute air shoved into her lungs,
   I wait by the bed in a chair positioned for her
   to see, should she, my face asking for the honest
   lively rise of what was always inside.

3. The priest came to the hospital. He invited me
   to mass's scorch. This too shall pass; there shall
   be weeping and gnashing of teeth as human law.
   As the priest talked, she chomped on the tube.
   Oil dripped from her eyes. I said, "Father, yes.
   It has been a lifetime since my last." On Sunday
   at St. Vincent de Paul, her pew empty, the church
   full of the old, the sick, and the small, I crossed
   my chest on this sixth Sunday of Easter, Jesus
   splayed on the wood, Mary standing on the earth.

Floating in drug-space or face in the dirt, who
chooses their faith, and what is it worth? In supportive
delirium, do we pray with our bodies bent over the bed?
Do the dead recognize the dead? Do we genuflect
to prove we can yet stand? I stood in the aisle, following
the communion line. Hands clasped in front, I took
the bread. On my mouth, the body for my body
dissolved and was gone: mother's hand, her step,
or her dress in an old chair. I walked past Mary's
statue. She wore a blue robe. Father Weir chanted
to God as I mouthed a refrain.

4. In the hospital of no soul's address,
of monitors, lines, infinite regress,
common now and at the hour of my mother,
the hour of ordinary Sundays and ordinary song.
Forget the fasts of Lent. Who kept for you?
Index drowning in the fount, I sing:
who calls us back to ourselves?

The air bed's circulatory roar pushes past the wake.
Angels come to ground, custodians sweeping
the tile with stone hair. A chart scatters
the message of name. We pray with our bodies
in the language of pain.

Diane Attwell Palfrey

Before and After
(01/21/1910)

A small child plays
in spirits' cockcrow hours.
One side of her pinafore bloody,
winterkill holds her breath
amid soft mutterings about noise,
big, scary noise. She leads
mediums to her marker
palled with grime, sings her age
in metered time . . .
3 years, 10 months, 26 days —
pressed against an angel's foot.

There is a hum, a vintage train telescopes.
Some cars burn on impact,
others topple into the Spanish River.
Survivors become seals on ice cakes.
The river is an orca, hungry for entremets.

Their focus draws back
to the little girl, such playfulness,
her pale pink pinny, unblemished now.
She skips around gravestones,
runs through spring grasses
in a game of tag. An Ojibway boy
loses one moccasin when he tries
to outrun her. Shadows of Indigo children
step from trees into this time —
this space.

NOTE: *The Spanish River derailment was one of the worst train accidents in Canadian history. The train jumped the tracks as it approached the railway crossing at the Spanish River near the settlement of Nairn in Northern Ontario near Sudbury.*

Brian Palmu

Canron Steel

Silver rectangular lakes
wait in eight-hundred degree
molten zinc holds. Towering
walls blister with exploded dross
in blunted sideways stalactites that waver
through pickling steam against
surgical wattage like scales
from a radiated B movie ogre.
But this is no movie,
and pulling away crusty zinc patches
as toupees for excitable Gary
got old by day two.

Crane hooks hang,
upended question marks.
Acid tank fumes chew me
with olfactory tattoos. Already
sweating before December's midnight start,
I scoop a galvanized hex bolt,
jab the wonky dispenser,
and inhale a handful
of blue salt tablets.
A skin-hidden lifer saunters,
lunchbox thermos of beer crooked
under arm, past a tagged steel beam,
and lights his smoke with his smoke.

A shiny-soled exec, newly-purchased
hard hat gleaming above
a slate blazer on his two-minute
walk-through at shift change, joked
at our crew. Now he saws to
and fro from a clogged glottis,
exuding Aqua Velva,
Rothman's and lemon gin.

Seven tons and hours later,
a perfect yellow circle, past
track-rows of floodlights,
transitions, through a cooling
beam's steam, to the serrated
border of a melanoma.

Deborah Panko

Hummingbird

Native Indian symbol for healing,
hummingbird
pulls north, south, east and west up
into her wings — a blur of looping eights

hovers for a moment
above pebbled path and dusty shoes,
her nectar-drenched beak
targeting my tie-dyed T-shirt.

We are walking
silently, somewhere
on Mt. Shasta in Northern California
through a garden of iron sculptures

wartime scenes from Vietnam
visited like stations of the cross
— before me a soldier carried on a stretcher
led by a nurse holding a lamp.

All metal to withstand the heat
the eroding wind,
these sculptures honour the sacrifice
but mostly call on regret.

Glitter of green wings, an arrow
in slow motion, hummingbird
touches down on the yellow creosote bush
on the impenetrable soldier clinging to life

circles the rainbow swirls of my summer top
rounding up fragments of this unfinished story . . . then,
our hearts pinned to the altar of heroic humanity,
vanishes into the blue.

Chris Pannell

Water Lilies
    for Janice Jackson

The tour group scatters across my view
of the pond like raucous brown and blue leaves
blown down. They slow and loosely gather —
chatter, laugh, and carelessly attend the
the echo
of their tour guide.
(Except one incessant giggler who cannot be still.)

Within l'Orangerie the climate control
is far too subtle to influence these
twelve around our seat.

Begone!
that I might sit selfishly with Monet's
curves, the walls, the work —
that I might fall into his mind
with my astonishment.
Then your warm fingers, and the invisible sun
touch my aching back, and reassure me
of the clouds.

I remember Ophelia —
how John Everett Millais kept her alive
      afloat in a bower of green, brightly erotic.

Today Monet's pond and sky are blessing blue
and absent the girl, he brings to mind the living lilies
and bamboo
of Giverny, his home, where we were
yesterday.

                                                                                                   >>>

Painted fronds move in my eyes —
or am I moved to see reflections of them in those clouds?
As if I float on the surface of all things
under shadow of willow
on wounds we have received
by rushing through
                what we came for
                      and might love
                              if only we would wait.

The tour group begins to leave
before their leader has finished her
forty-second song
about what they should see.
They know her refrain: *keep up, keep up!*

Time and my eyes widen on the foliage,
fronds. Weeds and puckers of pink,
deep greens underwater —
under skin, seem to snare and submerge us
(and Ophelia, again). Blooms pop white —
rush in from river bank, from the sky
to save us. So many places to rest
dans le jardin d'eau.

A Day Trip to El Alamein

The desert is full: small succulents, scorpions
Egyptian cobras, the horned viper —
and in the Commonwealth Soldiers' cemetery
a garden of cacti thrives.
Elsewhere the war has not been tidied up —
buried men beside their half-buried machines.
A Spitfire, a ration tin, spent shell casings
a uniform with its soldier blown out.
Here lies a sergeant of this war, known unto God.

El Alamein was a battlefield that is all museum
(until the day those luxury beach-side condos are finished).

On the way back to Cairo through the desert
we slow for hundreds of sheep crossing
and a Bedouin herder, who allows us to take his picture,
unconcerned with being paid.
This long, pristine asphalt ribbon
leads to the most crowded
city in the world: Cairo the triumphal, the ancient.

In the desert, I feel a small purification at losing
faith in our tour representative, who is now silent
after deceiving us several times and our driver
whose eyes are rooted to the road, his gaze as *steely*
as his new tires.

We do not have forty days to spare for fasting
or time to stop and purge behind the rear bumper —
We have only a photo of a soldier's cross
while solitude, sun, and sand remake the world
ecstatic and thin. I ignore repeated offers to stop
for bottled water allegedly imported
from foreign places like Canada. I will draw
on my internal fats and minerals
until I shed my bitterness
like a snake's skin
against that rock.

Gianna Patriarca

Italian Women

> *listen to our women*
> *the silence they make*
> *- Rocco Scotellaro*

these are the women
who were born to give birth

they breathe only
leftover air
and speak only
when deeper voices
have fallen asleep

i have seen them bleed
in the dark
hiding the stains inside them
like sins
apologizing

i have seen them wrap their souls
around their children
and serve their own hearts
in a meal they never
share

Returning

we don't discuss the distance anymore
returning is now
the other dream
not American at all
not Canadian or Italian
it has lost its nationality.

in the sixties we came in swarms
like summer bees
smelling of something strange
wearing the last moist kiss
of our own sky.
we came with heavy trunks
empty pockets
and a dream.

I was one of them
tucked away below the sea line
on the bottom floor of a ship
that swelled and ached
for thirteen days
our bellies emptied into the Atlantic
until the ship finally vomited
on the shores of Halifax
there, where the arms and legs
of my doll fell apart into the sea
finding their way back over the waves.

my mother's young heart wrapped around me
my sister crying for bread and *mortadella*
we held on
two more nights on a stiff, cold train
headed for Toronto
where the open arms of a half forgotten man
waited.

Nolan Natasha Pike

Forks of the Credit River

We used to twist my car
around the river
off Highway 10.
Way way up
the chunky planks of the
train bridge, running,

broken
ankles in my mind —
Stand By Me —
it feels like the movies in this valley.

The daring of being young
that I never had.
Never jumping,
always holding.

Twisting around the same river
its bank, romantic.
Our feet in the water
like Tom and Huck —
a couple of girls.

I could tell you anything,
even the time I lied
about getting punched
in the face
to keep her from leaving.

That maple bent over
from the other side,
its fingers dragging
in the water.

Our feet in the river,
jeans rolled,
handsome,
a couple of girls.

Stella Mazur Preda

The Tolling of the Bell
*St. James Church, Charlottetown, P.E.I.,
- October 7, 1859*

At the precise moment that night and day
cross celestial paths
three times tolls the belfry tower bell
splintering the chasm of stagnant silence.
Bewildered church neighbours
scramble out of foggy dreams;
trepidation and fear in every footstep.
Vintage church doors gape open
as if raped by tempestuous fall winds.
Like fallen stars from heaven
three womanly chiffon apparitions
illuminate the nave of the church,
halt the erratic onslaught of neighbours,
then meld into the slate darkness of early dawn.
Then — five more ominous staccatos of the bell.
Racing to the belfry, the townsfolk find no one.

Days later, comes the news —
the Fairie Queene has gone down.
Among the dead, eight passengers —
five men
three women

Robert Priest

Poem for a Tall Woman

If you have ever seen the green in water that is forever flowing out to mystery and adventure then you know something of the colour of her eyes. I would not talk so foolishly but there is a space in me she steps into — a tall shadow, an absence that howls like a grave or a dead wind when she is not there. I am a fool for her, letting all of me be a mile-long night breeze if she is but a straw held up — a single golden hair I might rush over forever. I love Marsha Kirzner like the taste of my own spit, like my own blood in my veins, ready to melt in her heat like snow carried south and dropped in Pacific surges, my mouth dissolved in tropical mangoes and sweet papaya. She is another tall self I keep inside and lean on like a prop — a magic self that sets me whirling and dispersing — an anchoring self like a two-ton idol thin and heavy in the bed, me fastened to it like a small burnt lizard. Let me just hold this mantis woman in my arms, this tall beautiful fire with green eyes. Let me just lick the length of this green blade, this lightning filament of her love and I will sizzle with it, a long green furrow in my spirit where a jade lake reaches for the peaks. Her hand is a leaf that can calm the passage of a storm and yet it is a leaf that sings in its work like a reed made of human flesh, a musical flesh of gasps and sighs — a high sweet strand of water like a violin string. Aaaah draw the bow down again my loved one across the heart, across the soul, draw the bow down again and play forever the long sweet notes of our love.

Brian Purdy

'basturd injuns'
    iambics for a battered race

Spat upon by us as 'basturd injuns'
Primitive in outlook, doomed to fail
They yet slip past our wampum logarithms
Seize their sky-fringed lances — and jump bail.

Restore to them the mansions of their fathers
Return to needled trees those naked stumps
Pull down your pride, embrace our secret brothers
A bear-claw pierce this heart if you deny.

Their blood's in every river with teeming fish
Their women stitched blue mountains to the sky
Turn our faces from them, they must vanish
But know, without their blood we wander blind.

masks - *David Haskins*

Kathy Robertson

Lest We Forget

Our shameful past exposed
as surely as whip
on slavery's backside
a tale that begs awareness —
segregation sewn
into Canada's fabric
by threads of bigotry.

> November 8, 1946
> Halifax businesswoman
> black civil rights pioneer
> sits in movie theatre's
> whites only section
> New Glasgow, Nova Scotia
> sleepy town on banks of East River
> forcibly removed   injuring hip
> incarcerated overnight
> denied legal counsel
> ghoulish shadows threaten
> to lynch vulnerability
> maintains composure
> back erect   white gloves in place
> convicted of criminal offense
> defrauding province one penny
> discrepancy of upstairs/downstairs admission
> plus, twenty-dollar fine; six-dollar court fee.

Yet undeterred
she mentors black women
her examples of dignity, grace, courage —
qualities for all to exemplify —
loosen stitches on historical quilt
her name spoken with pride:

> Viola Desmond
> first Canadian woman
> portrayed on ten-dollar bill.

Denis Robillard

The Body Sublime
    for Joyce

I am bothered all night
by the shape of my hands
The constant gurgles
of my recalcitrant heart.
I worry how light plays
timidly on your face
And how maybe one day
I will lose you too.

For now our bodies
assume old habits
We fall back
into the convenience
of the flesh
Reaching out now
for your touch
Building another bridge
to our unflinching allegiance.

Our lips meet softly
in the dark
Begin to share and co-mingle
in their silent taste
Like we have done
a thousand times before.

We do not speak
of the heart bereft
Of fathers and relatives
we have both lost.
There is a slow silent healing
the way our bodies
Are shared here.

O how I yearn
for your most charitable bones
How we both ponder
this breathing inside ourselves
After the afterglow.
After such a night
of chemical absorption
After this ecstatic tangle
of limbs.

In our own private forests
We climb into
one another's body
Like a luxuriant animal
Waiting for morning
to burst alive.

Kate Rogers

In the Dark, Age Eight after My Screams Wake Me

I wait for the creak
of bed springs down
the hall. Hear
nothing. Drop my pillow to
the floor, lower myself carefully
onto its snow drift. Wait to
sink before I slide.
My arms are ski poles.
Push, glide. Silence is
the other mouth breather
in this house. Gaping,
it swallows the tick of the furnace,
hum of the fridge.

Through mother's open door
I watch her in the blanket cocoon
arms around herself, clinging
like wings folded tight.

My sister is tucked in her bed
behind a plush barricade,
toothless lions and bears.

The light from father's study
puddles under his door.
Who will clean the stain off the floor?

Linda Rogers

Crow Revival, Second Line Beatitudes

Murder's come to recruit
for the Good Book,
chapter two, the music of
slaves, with pictures

by an artist who looked
at the sun without fear,
her fingers spread apart,
hands listening while
crow sisters opened up
their umbrellas, wings,
rapturing in little black
dresses, the sound of
skirts dipped in smudge,

filling the yonder with smoke,
charcoal warnings and blessings,

light fantastic.

Blessed are humans made of
clay and celestial longing.
Blessed are ribs scavenged by
Corvids, transformed into flutes
that are not afraid to be heard.

A Blessing

This is her blessing, world without end, one story after the other, every one in a different key. She's all ears, tucked in, curled up in her *capsula mundi*, ready for lift off, the rapture, maybe to a sacred forest, her former selves, nurselogs, rotting, *panis angelicus*; the holy *terroir*, her sinister smalldogs, little feet turning out, stirring up what comes next. She's swallowed her fairy suitcase, filled with baby teeth, waits for her cue, the obladi/ oblada aubade, morningsong. It's always morning, always the twitter of birds waking up, the idea of stretching into new bodies, this time, she hopes, an evergreen, her roots eating through compost, secrets and lies shared by the trickster, while her leaves reach up to the light. This time, she prays in her pervious shell, let's forgo consonants. This time, let's embrace the legato of vowels, the locus of beautiful dances, Sufis and ballerinas, green shoes growing like vines, Pinocchio's nose. Who will be the new fact checker, the puppet or the ventriloquist? Who will be the new whisperer, Crow again, really, or maybe cosmic lips, goddesses moving her branches? She loves it when green sticks sing, children in playgrounds, a mumuration of swallows, crows throwing their voices. La la how life goes on. Inside the newtree, She.

Karen Shenfeld

Woman at the River, Washing

Wherever the stream winds
past the village,
finding its way through a
queen-sized bed of rock

or swollen tributary lumbers
through shadows of copal,
laureate leaves.
Wherever the wadi leaps

to furious life,
you will find her.
You may call her Susanna,
but she is more likely

Yasmin or Kadidia, and
it is not her own self
she has come to wash clean.
Propped on the bank,

clothes pile the basket,
calling her attention
with their varied weights:
Dutch waxed prints

with which she wraps
the narrows of her waist
or straps a milk-drunk baby
to her back;

torn shorts and t-shirts
bearing worn-out words in
far-away tongues.
You have no business

watching her, but do.
She wades calf-deep,
the river watering
the hem of her garb,

gives each shirt, skirt,
pair of pants, a baptismal dip,
sudses them with
a shrunken bar, then

beats all hell out of them,
the slap of cloth
misting blue air
above her washboard —

a flat stone her mother
set at a slate's solid angle.
Caught in the power
of her moment,

you ache to think
how long she must bend,
her breasts drawn
to earth's core,

muscles flexed beneath
sweat-polished skin.
She rinses each charge
in turn, the current massaging

stray sleeves and legs,
battling her grip.
With a bold twist,
wrings a fine rain, then

lays her sodden cottons out,
in a dry, sunned spot,
the soap of angels
descending downstream.

Weatherman

Leaves of cloud
cast against
a porcelain sky.

Haloes 'round
the angel moon.

You took stock:
sun, wind, vapour,
the weight of air;

earth spinning on
its axis
beneath your rooted feet.

More than Abraham's,
you were Aristotle's scion:
your prophesies —

patterns perceived
in all that's connected,
in perpetual flux.

      *

Eight years to the day
(Eight years! Can it be?),

I mark the day you left:

thirteen below; the wind, northwest;

over Toronto towers,
your boyhood's prairie sky.

In the cemetery:
your impossible grave dug
in solid frozen ground.

      *

My palm grows warm
above the candle's small flame.

Weatherman!
What will tomorrow bring?

Milestones

Born in '56, this year, I turn 56. A scrap of fact
that seems, at least to me, significant.

In 1956, you turned 26: a married mother,
barricaded in a dry-walled suburb.

At 26, I rode a truck all night
from Karima to Khartoum.

I was 36 before I held my baby in my arms.
At that age you returned to work drilling

and filling teeth. I went back a day after giving birth
(if you can call writing poems for no money work).

What other milestones could we compare?
Well, you married at 24; I at 28.

(At 28, you bore your second child;
I produced but a single son.)

You lost your father at 32; Mine (your husband, yes,
I know, of 50 years) at 48. You retired at 65 . . .

Time is serpentine. A three-headed god
that split the primal world asunder. Mother,

you are as you were: 26 years older than me.
The distance between us narrows.

This is not a mirage. In time-lapsed frames,
Your lines crease my face. I lean on your cane.

Glen Sorestad

Blue Crabs, Galveston Bay

She slowly swings her woven circular net
into the Gulf that sloshes against rock slabs
of the elongated jetty on Bolivar Peninsula.

We stood, attentive to this tiny Asian crone,
while she knotted, as her ancestors taught,
a chunk of raw chicken into the mesh.

Further along the jetty, her two greying sons
cast lines into the bay, fiberglass surf rods,
afternoon sun flashing on expensive reels.

Now, crab trap at rest in the watery murk,
she sits back, content, on her rock to wait,
to sense movement below the rising tide.

We, too, wait and watch, curious, imagine
her great-grandfather whispering in her ear
minute details of foraging food from the sea.

The old woman rises, grasps the rope, draws
her net to the surface. *Aii-eee! A good one!*
She flips a large blue crab into the bucket.

Banana Loaf and Two Small Oranges
    for Naomi

this unexpected gift
nestled in a small
brown paper bag

banana loaf: a slab,
delectable and aromatic
its paper wrap a skin

two mandarin-sized oranges:
subdued colour, seeded,
assertive with tartness

everyday treasures
giver, gift, recipient
merged as one

A Straightener of Nails

Whenever my father spotted a nail, bent or twisted
by errant hammer, discarded as useless because it was
no longer true, he always picked up the reject to carry

along with him to where he kept an old tobacco can,
where the off-kilter joined the collection of cripples
needing his attention. It was a task for another day.

I was too young to understand his reason for doing this,
nor to fathom what satisfaction he received for his
slow and deliberate care, returning each nail to true.

This was when my father's livelihood was driving
his car down gravel or dirt roads selling Fuller brushes,
then Electrolux vacuums, Nutty Club confections.

He eked a meagre wage, but his heart was never in it.
His honesty and regard for others road-blocked sales
targets and he could never pressure anyone to buy.

On rainy weekends, I would find him in the workshop
happy with his hammer and his tobacco can, working
against time to set things right, the only way left to him.

Ken Stange

Learn To Appreciate Doors

> *"Which came out of the opened door — the lady or the tiger?"*
> Frank Richard Stockton ("The Lady or The Tiger")

They are extremely important to a traveller:
they let things in;
they let things out.
.

The variety is virtually infinite . with differences
both subtle and flagrant,
and the knowledgeable traveller can identify
at least a hundred major types.
.

The primary division . (the plant and animal
of door taxonomy) . is Phylum Open
and Phylum Closed.
.

Now, closed doors deserve more attention
than is usually afforded them
for they are mysterious in a way
a wall can only hope to be.
Not only do you not know
what lies beyond . (the lady or the tiger?)
but you don't know
if you want to know
and even then . if you try to open it
whether it will be locked . (and should you be glad?)
or not . (or not?)
.

(Incidentally, remember the smoke warning:
touch the door first,
if it is hot . don't open it.)
.

For example, think about bedroom doors:
Will the woman you love be there?
waiting for you?
or with your best friend?
.
Or closet doors:
consider the probability of skeletons.
.
Or cellar doors:
recall old horror movies.

And there is also the ambivalence of knocking:
ghosts knock;
so does opportunity.
.
However it should be mentioned that open doors
really are the more treacherous:
they invite entry,
assure one with partial in-sight,
but thresholds
are thresholds;
once crossed,
crossed.
.
Yet all this cautionary advice aside:
remember that windows are merely vicarious
and you . are . a traveller.

J.J. Steinfeld

Where You Get Lost or Go Astray

Walking among the city buildings
they turning into trees and the memory of trees
I think building-less thoughts
half-philosophical, half-recuperative:
where you get lost or go astray
where you court madness
or search for the abandoned
are the geographical underpinnings
of memory and self and biography
unwritten, spoken in code
adroitness in the words and pauses
and preparation for remembering
as you go deeper and deeper
into those old woods
woods that resembled a darkened city
what, you couldn't have been much more than twenty
so many things not to touch or eat
so many things that had no concern for you
except to scurry out of your way
or criticize you from a distance
in unfamiliar language.
Did the fox point a rifle at you?
Was the owl recording your steps?
You bring the dissatisfaction with you
and it misaligns your view.
You walked up to a skyscraper
and it was a tree that mocked your hapless identification.
The car that made you jump from street
to pile of decaying leaves
the driver was a friend of fox and owl
without remorse or compunction
only a beauty as natural as night
you found your way out
the skyscraper welcoming you home
the police officer taking the information
for the missing-person's report
looked somewhat like an owl
and you mention that
but too softly for anyone to hear.

Dane Swan

From these eyes

living the luxury of two jobs,
media overload,
mortgage payments,
bills, more bills,
and taxes —
the West isn't always
a capitalist paradise.

Join me.

I'll be the one
visiting story-tellers in trench-towns,
the guy learning new languages
by locals who teach curse words first.

We'll break bread with just our hands,
trying to explain to our new family
why rich people use two spoons,
three forks to eat a meal.

Try to see
through human eyes —
put our prejudice aside,
talk in terms of *us* instead of *they*.
Learn lessons through the art of conversation.

Find paradise.
Never return.

Blackface

Petty frauds
masquerading misery.
Watch them tap-dance —
dressed as hobos;
false smiles and shimmies
seek your pity, your money.

They are not *the real McCoy.*

Witness the genuine dance.
Watch how the soul propels —
a pulse that moves the congregation
like an ancient tsunami of legend.
You will fall down —
may never stand back up —
because this is our bedrock.

Our savage sophistication
flows through the earth
like the energy of a Juju man.
You are now observing
trance inducing moments —
the seizures are nothing to fear.

See us levitate while standing
on solid ground;
awe-struck like the first time
humanity heard Mahalia wail.
Follow us on the dirt path
to a shack at the crossroads.

Take a glimpse inside.

Experience our truth.

A culture constructed
by stolen people
who remember this dance
despite the whips and chains.
. . . this music
despite the lynchings.
. . . this art despite the prisons,
slave ships, ghettos,
miseducation.

The system designed to squash us
we thrive through —
Do not mistake us for weak.
Like the pillars that bound Samson,
some things were destined to crumble.
We have mastered
the art of impossible —
some swore we were devils —
we should have fallen ages ago.

You'll be disappointed
if you thought
we'd shuck and jive on cue —
this dance is not for your entertainment.

This is a celebration,
a hallelujah,
a thank you to our ancestors,
a kiss to our mother who has
blessed our toil filled journey.

You're more than welcome to
join us on this trail.

Lynn Tait

Slipstream

> *We are all made up fragments, so shapelessly and strangely assembled that every moment, every piece plays its own game. And there is as much difference between ourselves and ourselves as between us and others.*
> - Montaigne

She drifts into various life forms,
enters unnoticed through separate doors,
assumes the shape of masks,
stained-glass and candles
so she might see herself aflame,
reflect on her ability to grow soft and small,
provide light to fit and fuse harlequin elements —
pieces of persona contoured and shaded.

Avoiding liaisons black with holes,
she shifts into sound waves,
gains access to conversations
clinging to the sides of diphthongs
that drop dangerous and sudden
into hard letters, unsigned, cut short —
each long sound bears with it an uncomfortable silence,
no one able to comment on her painful transitions,
the energy needed to sustain each form.

When time permits,
she covers herself with moss
softening the violence of flight,
listens for ripples in the atmosphere,
waits for the proper slipstream
to carry her, back to the place
where a slight turn of her head
altered the course of planets.

Fishing in South-east Ontario

Something between a sport and a religion
         - Josephine Tey "The Singing Sands"

Family said I'd never have the patience.
I was wasting my time.
The admonishment rippled and chopped,
the sound of carp kissing air.
I thread worms on hooks like popcorn on string.

Along the shallows, my brothers
claim better bait, bigger fish,
over-turn rocks, disturb sand and silt,
scrounge for crayfish that skitter-scatter
gray against a liquid terrain.

I'm content catching perch with bologna bits,
worms for rock bass; and sunfish,
dorsal bristling like finned cats
I step on lightly, my hands too small
to wrangle out hooks by any other means.

At Grandpa's cottage, we travel by boat.
I'm warned trolling fingers, easy snack for pike.
Brothers laugh when I exclaim I've caught a *loud*-mouth bass.
The water like mica flecks reflects the sun as moving rocks,
or the fin flicks of shiners slithering in perforated pails.

In winter, across a still-life horizon of white ice,
make-shift shacks pepper the lake-scape
like thick brushstrokes placed wherever.

Within this canvas, sheltered anglers
huddle over small circles of lake,
softly tickling cut-out ice edges,
hooks and breath baited,
wait for silent tugs,
the zip of line and reel,
the sudden stir of silver
slashing deep through blue-black currents,
pulling away from the choking light.

Jennifer Tan

Still

Stay beside my still water,
drink in me.

My skin, my smile and my soft voice drew you to me.
You were thirsty for me,
you were tempted to drink me into your blood
but when the dark cloud hung over us like a gloomy tree,
it turned me less lovely in your eyes.
You saw me dressed in another shade,
a disturbance on the smooth surface of my skin.

As you wet your face,
you would not lick me with your tongue
and drink to your fill.
You would not give in to change.

I am still water
wanting you to take me in,
to slake your thirst.
I want you to remember me as you first saw me
without the cloudy interception of doubt
that discolored me and pulled you away.

I will call you again to stay,
to run your fingers over my skin
to break the tension, move me, change me
Watch me surface through for you.

Stay still beside me,
drink in my water.

The Wind Chime

you hang the wind chime on the clothes line
wait for the wind
the sounds that awaken your mind

to the cling of sweat on your back when it is hot
or to the sucking of clay at your feet when it is wet

to Sumatra and Java,
wayang kulit and *Sanskrit*
dukun and *pantun*

Indonesian bamboo music imbues and echoes
a trance on the trail of a dance

crow - *Elana Wolff*

Grace Vermeer

Returning To Fairpoint, Ohio

i.

Do you remember
the white clapboard church by the tracks?
The black-roofed belfry with its slatted windows
rose above double doors,
but in the four years we lived there,
the bell never rang —
    Was it missing?

I traveled back to Fairpoint
along narrow roads, winding past abandoned shafts,
shabby houses clinging to hillsides.
I stopped at the bend that heads into town
and took a photograph of the church.

I was thinking about the girl I was,
hung like a bell without a tongue.
When I looked out over coal-ravaged hills,
I heard voices like bells.
    One of those voices was mine.

ii.

God of the lost and forgotten
coal mining towns
scattered along Ohio's state roads.

God of my father refusing his future
at First National Bank, turning his back
on Allegheny College, choosing
the church that sat thirty yards from the tracks —

    Have mercy.

He paused his sermon at 11:51 every Sunday
for the shrill whistle crossing, coal cars rumbling,
flattening pennies we'd left on the tracks.

    >>>

God of his sighs every Friday
while miners cashed pay checks at Piatek's Night Club.
The shouts, shattering glass and jukebox tunes
wafted through my window on hot July nights.

God of my mother in the rambling parsonage,
who whistled like a cardinal
when nothing was fine with six children
and red headed Eleanor moving in, epileptic, pregnant at 40,
she climbed up on the dining room table
and my mother cried, *No! No! Come down!*
Eleanor crashed in a willowy heap
and everything was fine, just fine.

God of my two older brothers who learned to trap muskrats
and shoot out the town's three streetlights with Bill's .22
then sat alone in opposite pews for ten Sundays
under my father's stern eye.

God of the Mennonite church
with its handsome black families, Italians and Greeks, Polish Catholics
who abandoned the liturgy
for the common vernacular and a cappella hymns
unless Don Hoffman showed up
and leaned into the keys of the upright piano,
his face lit up with his gap-toothed grin,
his eyes following Leona as she led the songs.

God of the brown brick school on the hill
and vicious girls in sixth grade —
> *Forgive me for telling them*
> *my best friend Marcia wasn't wearing a bra.*

God of the teacher who kicked Fred down the stairs
then propped his feet on the desk and wiped chalk off his hands —

> *Have mercy.*

God of slag heaps and buckeye trees,
Sulfur Creek running red-orange and muddy
while dump trucks ground gears and grit drifted down
on flannel diapers flapping on clotheslines.

God of coal companies that scalped the land
then stocked bass in strip pits, planted crown vetch
and gave Gary a glass eye and a new trailer
after he survived the explosion,
coal flecks still embedded in his cheeks.

God of the girl who learned not to talk,
who leaned out of her top story window
watching the lights of Big Musky devour the hills
night after night —

   Have mercy.

She didn't know her eyes were deep wells
and the voices, the laughter,
the gritty sounds of the town
were falling like rocks
into deep water inside her,
she didn't know rocks will cry out
and stones will tell stories.

iii.

I am trying to say the scarred landscape
and the Sunday ghost voices
followed me for six thousand miles and twenty odd years
till I turned and crawled back
into the bones of the girl I'd deserted,
becoming a woman resuscitated from her dead life.

I've returned to the town
and now stand in the gravel in front of the church,
gathering years in my arms,
lifting them up by the tracks
across from Nicolozake's Café.

I am saying, This was my life
and I want it.

The Monks of Skellig Michael

No sail, no rudder, just our lives
adrift, offered to the one who speaks

to wind, salt-spray and waves —
the current sucks us further out.

No questions in the early hours,
our ears unstopped, our hearts

all soft and listening, our wounds
tied in a leather sack.

      *

A crane flies low — it also seeks
a harbor, shore —

we circle in this liminal space,
a labyrinth of water.

This is the great and holy dark
that spins the stars, each one

ordained and named.

      *

On this tiny desolate peak
we chisel rock, ascending steps

slick from the sea, our home
we stacked from stones,

shaped like cones or beehives, but
no honey here or gold applause,

no voice that says, Well done.
No, heaven presses hard,

bone cold I stand in rotting clothes
and watch for God.

Ghazal For Eve's Daughters

Some women resist ruin for three thousand years.
The wrecking ball smashes the front closet and hall
but they just keep humming and dusting the knick-knacks.

Lot's wife disobeyed, turned and looked back at what was
forbidden. Now she refuses to risk any tears.
She's afraid four tears might dissolve her salt pillar.

I watched a woman sell everything for one gleaming pearl.
When the man in the death-hat drove up to her door,
she refused his offer of thirty more years.

In my dreams I keep looking for windows and light.
Yesterday I read about Barbara, locked in a tower,
she traded her life for the light from three windows.

Pascal pulled out his theory of probability,
threw the dice on the table and said, Let's bet.
Why did he think I had nothing to lose?

When the truck broke down in Montana, I left
my soul by the side of the road, near a ditch.
Years later I opened a wound, the soul slipped back in.

One Cup Holds Twenty Thousand Small Wonders
   for Issa (1763-1828)

You came into the world
as everyone does, hungry,
clutching a litany of wishes,
but you were a sparrow

pushed out of the nest
by a stepmother who left
you to care for the baby,
your clothes wet with urine.

You wandered through fields,
country temples and bells,
bent to peer at the lowest
creatures, mosquitoes, fleas,

a slow-footed snail,
or the locusts' shrill song,
a brown mottled toad
squatting among fallen blossoms.

But fate whittled and cut
and never stopped taking —
your wife, your four children,
your health and your house swept by fire.

You chose the name *Issa* —
one cup of tea —
as if you had stripped your desire
till you found one glowing ember

and with your breath
fostered a flame that became
twenty thousand small wonders,
each a lit candle, set on a hill.

Two hundred years later
your tiny haiku
shine through the door of my ruin.
You show me one life

and with that flicker of light,
I distill my desire,
lift the cup I am given
and walk through the burnt door.

Wendy Visser

News Flash

Those who think hell is hot
have never lived a Yukon winter
where the only warmth
is a sizzling fire, bottle of whisky,
and vivid imagination,
not coloured by drink,
but by conversations with yourself
in debates about temperature
and its proximity to hell.

Those who think that cleanliness
is next to godliness should pitch a tent
or hunker in a cabin where every day
you melt ice to drink, cook, wash.
Usually, the wash part is a damp rag
in fast rubs over your face.
Removal of clothes for a body scrub
is risky business, performed only
when the thermometer rises a few degrees,
or the itch from lice, or your own aroma
gets unbearable.

And so it is in this climate of cheek
and challenge that even God
doesn't venture out, though one miner
thinks he sees him cozy up to the bar
with other Saturday night regulars.
He persists in his belief and who knows.

We are a ragtag, bobtail crew
of seasoned sourdoughs
who do know where hell is
and we know that heaven
is a mountain of wood,
a hot bath and a clean shirt.

Fish Fry

Up and in the boat
when dawn lights the bow,
sound of fishing reels
stretch toward the horizon
while cast lines
as long as morning
float upon the water.
In day's haul
with fish on their sides
skins slit from head to tail
I think of my father
during shock treatments
and how he flip-flopped
like fish before gutting.
Done to burn off the depression —
as if orphaned young
then war-time soldiering
and lost suns
are surface things
an electric prod can fix.

When he comes home
he is just an ember
of his old self
floundering
the hook
still in his mouth.

Bruce Whiteman

Slightly Below Normal

The boys and girls, their spry and unbattered
bodies, who give hope to those of us whose glum
dismay feels overwhelming now, sit straight and

smiling, staring at nothing but each other. That's fine.
They're thinking green, progenitive thoughts,
and that's their inalienable lovely teenage

right. And lucky they. It doesn't last, not really,
and soon enough there's baby food to make from
scratch or importunate fortune, whatever form it is

that fortune takes. Blind luck, or down you go.
Out the Meeting House window leaves still
hang on trees. The wind is up and working

hard to turn the poplars naked. Everything
eventually falls and is revealed for what it is:
Queen-Anne's-lace a skein of thin brown veins

and friable seed-pods, most of the way to death,
milkweed shrinking inwards and likewise gone for
good, or gone at least into winter's coming

clutch for now, daisy fleabane only left to
cheer the disaffected and the grieved at heart,
white and sacrificial, moth-food, pure.

Elana Wolff

Messenger Suite

Loon

No one's remorse is like your remorse.
Even at the start of spring,
      that is to say
the start of love,
your call holds every memory of dejection.
And you think I have understood the source.

    Rook

    Feathers the colour of onyx,
    colour of toenails —
                black and bruised.
    Language coarse as curse.
    Blatant gaze, as if to say, *It's your turn*,
    meaning mine.
                I laugh and caw
    and caw again — struggling with this other tongue.
    Mine is hunkered states away.

                 In the garden,
    on my knees, I offer you some plum.
    This is how you came to jab my hand.

Goldfinch

Flitting left to left, the yellow light in twilight
gold. Soft at first,
then fulgent,   The fence can't intervene.
then the colour of curative music.   The yellow streams, its frequency
Song, a salve, floats over the field   a shift. Shadow, for a moment
and through the schoolyard fence.   trembles, making space for quiet:
                                                   motion for a confidential note.

                                                                         >>>

Red Bird

I hear you,
I know
you're near.

I do not expect you
to draw nearer.
I never expected to touch your body.

It is enough to behold —

And if you have chosen
to come to this garden,

and to return,

it is because you know
I know
to keep my distance.

Heron

Are you not the tall one who raised me up?
Potent:
        how you stand on the pond-rock,
your blue uniform investing authority,
even without the hat.

And none of the force that comes so often with power.

Sparrow

Your voice is back —
scratchy as thorns on glass.

Your other voice —
the one you keep for tenderness —
has gone to sleep.

Cheep, cheep.

Meaning, too little of you
to please me.

Gull

My lightness should be clear to you,
as yours is to me.
We are like enough in these bodies
to correspond.
I should know by now when you wake me up —
reeling and screaming out loud that way,

there are really two voices at work.
One that needs to cry out
and one that cries to be reached.

I'm listening. My gladness is your call,
though the hour is early
(or late),
though I never possess the food you need,
or answer.

Hummingbird

You say I'll get nothing but silence from you,
yet there you go — spinning your wings.
Is this simply how you're wired,
or is this your lullaby?

You are audible to me,
                even in absence.
Absence is only a physical thing.
I remain committed —

not for the sake of any impression,
though you do impress me. Yes —
I want this word to last.
If you don't believe, let me.   >>>

Canada Goose - *Elana Wolff*

Dove

A name that's come to stand for appeasement —
from the Old French word for peace.
Peace is pleasing.
      Appeasement, to you,
sounds like social control.
I give you that.
Definitions are often what we want,

yet we can't force clearness,
               let alone accord.
Even 'short neck' and 'stout beak'
can be matters of perception.

And even if words are measured,
gesture may give us away.

Dove is a Germanic
word that refers
to the bird's
diving flight.

Starling

Tell me: What is the difference
between infinity and eternity?
I've heard you trill these syllables —
you must have a feel for their sense.

Flock

I've seen in the northern garden:
sparrows, starlings, robins, rooks.
               Once there was a junco.

Now a pair of cardinals has taken to the space.

These birds — they must be messengers.
They've come.

Jan Wood

Shafts of Sun

take back the conversations
of a page, the blank calendar, the square root of crosswords
the tracks letters leave when they walk
across the daily news and a well-worn bible

dance in ballerina slippers
toes pointed in a leap of grace, trail feathers and fur
ripple like a cougar following its blood-music
belong to a flock, a herd, a naming of place

listen to the grass, the swish and tangle of brome
stringed instruments playing banjos in the wind
unwrap the scent of streams, taste raindrops in the dust
wear summer's aftershave

paint your tongue purple with the forest
lullabies and wildness, let small globes of gentian violet
explode earth in the wholeness of your mouth
the seed, the juice, its stain: a permanence

inhale the tobacco of reeds in a shaft of sun
sip deep notes of campfire coffee at the base of a jack pine
sit there until the sky spills its stars
and Venus is within reach

Ed Woods

Alzheimer's Lack of Compassion

Mom peers out entrance doors
awaiting my weekly visit
this image overpowers frustration
of congested traffic to Toronto
My disgust is sickening
for highway decision makers

Let us have visible benefits
of kickbacks and payola
to reach this building of compassionate souls
eager for contact and love
or a trip down memory lane

Walking into the Nursing Home
mom brightens up as a child opening gifts
I knew you would visit today

A waif in a wheelchair gets the royal tour
as if a new adventure
we pass many less fortunate guests
and find a quiet time to reminisce
Her war work years building Lancaster Bombers
for young aviators to defend freedom
many never came home
Military transfer to Montreal
to produce layout drawings
Bren guns, landing gears
or tank assembly schematics
sub zero marching around barracks
The antics of working the Toronto Film Festival
or a flight in my plane over Toronto
Her ride home in my transport truck
when stranded in a blizzard
and many long ago Sunday outings
until we drift into family happenings
and refreshing picture albums

Time is nigh for slumber
quietness seeps into the evening air
as darkness eliminates window panes
Mom begins to yawn
as we roll down the carpeted highway
to the last room on the right

Wheelchair brakes go on in the doorway
as mom pauses for one soft question
She didn't want to be troublesome today
as our time together is so special
but on my next visit would it be OK
if we went for a drive to Hamilton
so she could visit her son

Anna Yin

My Body Is a Flute

there are holes calling for music.
not like a piano
black and white keys
neatly displayed, altering its tune
by swift movement of fingers.

Instead, holes listen to your whispers,
carry them from winter to spring . . .
so many voices flow in and out,
make leaves changing color.

Last night I had that dream —
you came to play
the music so beautiful
the story so sad.

sunset - *Richard M. Grove*

ACKNOWLEDGEMENTS

The editor thanks his sweetheart, Norma West Linder, for proofreading *Tamaracks* as well as for her editorial erudition. Her suggestions are always valued.

Robert S. Acorn:
"Bedspread" and "Passchendaele" were initially published in *White Strawberries* (Charlottetown, Prince Edward Island: TWiG Publications, 2000).

Becky D. Alexander:
"Buried Deep" was initially published in the TOPS newsletter, 2004 and was later published in WRAC (Waterloo Regional Arts Council, 2005), and later still it was collected in *Cambridge Wartime Scrapbook*, 2005.

Rosemary Aubert:
"The Plague 1665 – 1666" was initially published in *Grain* in 2016.

Henry Beissel:
4 from: "Stones to Harvest" were initially published in *Stones to Harvest* (Goderich, Ontario: Moonstone Press, 1993).
"Manifesto in Times of War" and "Amaryllis" were collected in *Sightlines* (Toronto: Guernica Editions, 2016).

Nancy M. Bell:
"Henge" was initially published in *Through This Door* in 2010.

Steven Michael Berzensky (Mick Burrs):
"Breathing In the Bees", "Notes on Mandelstam", and "Heart" were initially collected in *Variations on the Birth of Jacob.* (Winnipeg: The Muses' Company, 1997).

Clara Blackwood:
"Persephone Unbound" was initially published in *Juniper* in 2017.

Robert A. Boates:
"Late September" and "The Good Life" will appear in *Man Without Memory: Poems New & Selected.*

Frances Boyle:
"Pelican Narrows" was initially published in *Contemporary Verse 2*, Summer 2006, and subsequently collected in *Light-carved Passages* (Ottawa: BuschekBooks 2014).

Mary Lee Bragg:
"My Mother's Birds" was initially published in *Winter Music* (Tree Press, 2013).

Allan Briesmaster:
"In Flight" was initially published in *Pod and Berry* (Thornhill, Ontario: Aeolus House, 2017).

Ronnie R. Brown:
"For Keeps" was initially published in *States of Matter* (Windsor, Ontario: Black Moss Press, 2005).
"Thoughts After The Carnage" was initially published in the annual *LUMMOX* anthology (San Pedro, California: Lummox Press, 2015).

Patrick Connors:
"Exit Poll" was initially published in *Envoy*, the newsletter of the Canada Cuba Literary Alliance, in 2014.

Tony Cosier:
"Saw Music" was initially published in *The Journal*.
"Stone Steps" was initially published in *Pennine Platform*.

Lorna Crozier:
"The Mask" – Excerpted from *The Wrong Cat* by Lorna Crozier. Copyright © 2015 by Lorna Crozier. Reprinted by permission of McClelland & Stewart, a division of Penguin Random House Canada Limited.
"Time Studies" was initially published in *What the Soul Doesn't Want* (Calgary: Freehand Books, 2017).
"My Last Erotic Poem" – Excerpted from *Small Mechanics* by Lorna Crozier. Copyright © 2011 by Lorna Crozier. Reprinted by permission of McClelland & Stewart, a division of Penguin Random House Canada Limited.
"The Underworld" was initially published in *What the Soul Doesn't Want* (Calgary: Freehand Books, 2017).

Phillip Crymble:
"Nursery" was initially published in *Burning Bush 2* and later collected in *Not Even Laughter* (Ennistymon, Ireland: Salmon Poetry, 2015).

James Deahl:
"Ulysses" was initially published in *Philadelphia Poets* and later collected in *Red Haws to Light the Field* (Toronto: Guernica Editions, 2017).

"Confronting The Idea Of The Good On A Rainy Night In Early May" was initially published in *Canadian Stories* and has been broadcast on TVCogeco.

"Silence In The Fields Of Autumn" was initially published in *California Quarterly* and later collected in *Two Paths Through The Seasons* (Metulla, Israel: Cyclamens and Swords Publishing, 2014).

G. W. Down:
"Trolling Toward Terror" was initially published in *Tower Poetry*.

Gertrude Olga Down:
"Babelplatz, Berlin" was initially published in *Tower Poetry*.

Jennifer Lynn Dunlop:
"Blue Delphiniums" was initially published in *Tower Poetry* in 2002.

Margaret Patricia Eaton:
"Sunflowers" and "Winter Woods" were initially published in *Vision & Voice* (Moncton, New Brunswick: Eagle Wings Press, 2011).

Daniela Elza:
"autobiography of grief   1" was initially published in *Prism international* in 2015.

Venera Fazio:
"Broken" was initially published in *Philadelphia Poets,* 2014 and later collected in *Scarlet Thistles, A Canadian anthology of Poetry* (Toronto: Beret Days/The Ontario Poetry Society, 2014).

Fran Figge:
"The Fault of the Apple" was initially published in *Tower Poetry* in 2017.

Doris Fiszer:
"In the Year Before She Died" and "Foraging" will be published in a chapbook by Bywords.

Kate Marshall Flaherty:
"Lost" was initially published in *Stone Soup* (Toronto: Quattro Books, 2014).

Jennifer L. Foster:
"Wild Apple Tree" and "In Snug Harbour, Georgian Bay" were initially published in *Tower Poetry*.

Linda Frank:
"A Long Time Coming" and "Chasing Shadows" were initially published in *Insomnie Blues* (Ottawa: BuschekBooks, 2011).
"You've Been On My Mind" was initially published in *Cobalt Moon Embrace* (Ottawa: BuschekBooks, 2002).

Ryan Gibbs:
"Daylight my Darknesses" was initially published in *Under the Mulberry Tree: Poems for & about Raymond Souster* (Toronto: Quattro Books, 2014).

Katherine L. Gordon:
"Leonardo's Flying Machine" was initially published in *Moonlight The Sky Will Slide* (Metulla, Israel: Cyclamens and Swords Publishing).
"Beowulf's Blade" was initially published in *Translating Shadows* (Cambridge, Ontario: Craigleigh Press).

Andreas Gripp:
"The West Coast of Somewhere" and "Marooning the Muse" are from his latest collection, *Panthera Leo*.

David Haskins:
"Resilience" was initially published in *Canada 150 - From Far and Wide: Multicultural Creative Writing Collection 2017* (Vancouver: WS Press, 2017).
"Reclamation" was initially published in *Canadian Forum* in 1978 and was later collected in *Reclamation* (Ottawa: Borealis Press, 1980), and later still in *This House Is Condemned* (Hamilton, Ontario: Wolsak & Wynn, 2013).

Eryn Hiscock:
"Harem (Ted Bundy Poem)" was initially published in *Descant*, Spring 2011.
"After *Frankenstein*" was initially published in *The Nashwaak Review*, 2012.

Laurence Hutchman:
La Dentellière was initially published in *Beyond Borders* (Fredericton, New Brunswick: Broken Jaw Press, 2000) and later collected in *Selected Poems* (Toronto: Guernica Editions, 2007), and later still in *The Artis* in 2017.
"Milkweed" was initially published in *Foreign National* (Ottawa: Agawa Press, 1993) and later collected in *Selected Poems* (Toronto: Guernica Editions, 2007).

Susan Ioannou:
"Mineralogy Lesson" was initially published in *TickleAce*, then in the *Dream Catcher*

(UK) Canadian Issue, and later it was collected in *Looking Through Stone* (Your Scrivener Press, 2007).

"Imagine That Greek Island" — an earlier version was initially published in *Women's Education des femmes* and later collected in *Looking for Light* (Brighton, Ontario: Hidden Brook Press, 2016).

I.B. Iskov:
"When He Died, He Took One Last Poem with Him" was initially published in *Earle Birney: A Tribute* (Vancouver: PRISM international, 1998).

Ellen S. Jaffe:
"Water Children" was initially published in *CV2* in 1999 and was later collected in *Water Children* (Hamilton, Ontario: Mini Mocho Press, 2002).

Maureen Korp:
"Friday afternoon" was initially published in *Anti-Terror and Peace* (Israel: IFLAC Word Press, 2016).

Donna Langevin:
"In the Café du Monde" and "If "Live Oaks" Could Laugh" were initially published in *In the Café du Monde* (Brighton, Ontario: Hidden Book Press, 2008) and later in *The Laundress of Time* (Thornhill, Ontario: Aeolus House, 2014).

John B. Lee:
"Bringing the Farmhouse Down" was initially published in *Descant* and later collected in *The Full Measure* (Windsor, Ontario: Black Moss Press, 2016).

"The Ungoable" was initially published in the anthology *Crossing Borders* (Brighton, Ontario: Hidden Brook Press, 2015) and was later collected in *This is How We See the World* (Brighton, Ontario: Hidden Brook Press, 2017).

"On kindness" will appear in *Beautiful Stupid* (Windsor, Ontario: Black Moss Press, 2018), as will both "Bringing the Farmhouse Down" and "The Ungoable".

Bernice Lever:
"Young Eyes Ask Why" was initially published in *Blessings* (Windsor, Ontario: Black Moss Press, 2000).

Norma West Linder:
"Little Boy Lost" was initially published in *Voices Israel*.

"Last Poem for Irving Layton" was initially published in *Adder's-tongues: A Choice of Norma West Linder's Poems, 1969 – 2011* (Thornhill, Ontario: Aeolus House, 2012).

Annick MacAskill:
"Tatiana in Gaspra, 1902" was initially published in *No Meeting Without Body* (Kentville, Nova Scotia: Gaspereau Press, 2018).

Blaine Marchand:
"In the White Giant's Thigh" was initially published in *The Craving of Knives* (Ottawa: BuschekBooks, 2010).
"Life is a Train" was initially published in *Arc Magazine*'s We All Begin in Little Magazines (1998) and was later collected in *The Craving of Knives* (Ottawa: BuschekBooks, 2010).
"Zakat" was initially published in *Aperture* (Ottawa: BuschekBooks, 2008).
"Song of Little Squirrel" was initially published in *Open Fires* (Perth, Ontario: Anthos Press, 1987).

Mori McCrae:
"Gravity" was initially published in *Passersby, Poems by Mori McCrae*, 2018.

Ian McCulloch:
"Carl Martin's Tongue Stuck To The Merry-Go-Round" was initially published in *Parables and Rain* (Ottawa: Penumbra Press, 1993).

Susan McMaster:
"Sign of Respect" was initially published in *Crossing Arcs: Alzheimer's, My Mother, and Me* (Windsor, Ontario: Black Moss, 2009, reprint 2010).
"How God sees" was initially published in *Uncommon Prayer: A book of dedications* (Kingston, Ontario: Quarry, 1997) and later in *Waging Peace: Poetry & Political Action* (Ottawa: Penumbra Press, 2002), and later still in *Paper Affair: Poems Selected & New* (Windsor, Ontario: Black Moss, 2010).

Lynda Monahan:
"taken away" was initially published in *Transition magazine* in 2015.

Colin Morton:
"Last Rites" was initially published on Ottawater.com (2015).

Marion Mutala:
"Seductress" was initially published in *Ukrainian Daughter's Dance* (Toronto: Inanna Publications, 2016).

Shane Neilson:
"Angelic Salutation" was initially published in *The Fiddlehead* and later collected in *Dysphoria* (Erin, Ontario: The Porcupine's Quill, 2017).

Diane Attwell Palfrey:
"Before and After" was initially published in *Simply Because We are Canadian* (The Cambridge Writers' Collective, 2017).

Brian Palmu:
"Canron Steel" was initially published in *Sunset Mathematics* (Frog Hollow Press, 2017).

Deborah Panko:
"Hummingbird" was initially published in *From O to Snow* (Brighton, Ontario: Hidden Brook Press, 2010).

Gianna Patriarca:
"Italian Women" and "Returning" were initially published in *Italian Women and Other Tragedies* (Toronto: Guernica Editions, 1994).

Nolan Natasha Pike:
"Forks of the Credit River" was initially published in *Event* in 2016.

Stella Mazur Preda:
"The Tolling of the Bell" was initially published in *Myth Weavers: Canadian Myths and Legends* (Waterdown, Ontario: Serengeti Press, 2007).

Robert Priest:
"Poem for a Tall Woman" was initially published in *The Man Who Broke out of the Letter X* (Toronto: Coach House Press, 1984).

Kathy Robertson:
"Lest We Forget" was initially published in *Simply Because We are Canadian* (The Cambridge Writers' Collective, 2017).

Karen Shenfeld:
"Woman at the River, Washing" was initially published in *Sparks* and later collected in *The Fertile Crescent* (Toronto: Guernica Editions, 2010).
"Weatherman" was initially published in the *Maple Tree Literary Supplement*.

Glen Sorestad:
"Blue Crabs, Galveston Bay" was initially published in *Dime Show Review* in 2017.
"Banana Loaf and Two Small Oranges" initially appeared in *Triadae Magazine* in 2017, published in both English and Spanish translation.
"A Straightener of Nails" was initially published in *The Duke City Fix*.

Ken Stange:
"Learn To Appreciate Doors" was initially published in *Advice To Travellers* (Ottawa: Penumbra Press, 1994).

J.J. Steinfeld:
"Where You Get Lost or Go Astray" was initially published online in *Abstract Magazine,* and a short fiction by the author of the same title based on this poem is included in *Madhouses in Heaven, Castles in Hell* (Victoria, British Columbia: Ekstasis Editions, 2015).

Dane Swan:
"From these eyes" and "Blackface" were initially published in *Bending the Continuum* (Toronto: Guernica Editions, 2011).

Lynn Tait:
"Slipstream" was initially published in *Quills Canadian Poetry Magazine* in 2006.
"Fishing in South-east Ontario" was initially published in *Cherish Our Heritage* (London, Ontario: HMS Press, 2004) and later collected in *Liaisons*: R. D. Lawrence Commemorative Anthology (Minden, Ontario: Haliburton Writers, 2007).

Jennifer Tan:
"Still" and "The Wind Chime" were initially published in *Tower Poetry*.

Grace Vermeer:
"Returning To Fairpoint, Ohio" - section i. was initially published as "Postcard to my Brother" in *Big Art Book* (Scarborough, Ontario: Scarborough Arts, 2014).

Wendy Visser:
"Fish Fry" was initially published in *Tower Poetry*.

All other poems appear in *Tamaracks* for the first time.

Can – National - *Lynn Tait*

CONTRIBUTORS

Robert S. Acorn was born in Charlottetown in 1927 and lives in Brackley, Prince Edward Island. He is a member of both the Prince Edward Island Writers' Guild and The Writers in Group (TWiG). Acorn has published both poetry and short stories. He also plays the saxophone.

By Robert S. Acorn: *White Strawberries* (Charlottetown, Prince Edward Island: TWiG Publications, 2000).

Sylvia Adams' publications include a novel, *This Weather of Hangmen*, a children's book, *Dinner at the Dog Pound*, and two poetry collections, *Sleeping on the Moon*, runner-up for the Archibald Lampman prize, and Cranberry Tree Press 1998 winner, *Mondrian's Elephant*. A book reviewer for several publications, including *Canadian Bookseller* and *Bywords*, former poetry editor for *The Ottawa Citizen*, writing instructor-facilitator in Canada and Chile, and editor/publisher as ADAR Press of chapbooks by her workshop groups, she is a founding member of Canada's Field Stone Poets, with poems appearing in their chapbooks and their travel collection, *Whistle for Jellyfish*. Her work appears in over thirty literary magazines including *Queen's Quarterly*, *Arc Poetry Magazine*, and League of Canadian Poets Vintage anthologies. Awards include Aesthetica's International Competitions (2012 and 2013), several Canadian Authors National Capital Region Contests and the Diana Brebner Prize. She is an introvert, synesthete, vegetarian, bibliophile, ailurophile, dedicated Luddite and one of the last Victorians.

By Sylvia Adams: *Whistle for Jellyfish* (BookLand Press, 2011), *Dinner at the Dog Pound* (Trafford Publishing, 2009), *Sleeping on the Moon* (Hagios Press, 2006), *Mondrian's Elephant* (Cranberry Tree Press, 1998), and *This Weather of Hangmen* (General Store Publishing House, 1996).

Becky D. Alexander was born and raised in Hespeler. She now resides in the Preston area of Cambridge, Ontario. She acquired her Bachelor of Arts degree at Wilfrid Laurier University and took post-graduate studies in education through the University of Western Ontario, where she acquired Specialist Certificates in Special Education and Visual Arts. Her writing has won hundreds of awards. She has been published in five provinces, twenty-two of the United States and in six countries. Becky won first place in the Canadian Authors Associations (the George Cadogan Award for Excellence in Writing, 1997) from the Waterloo Wellington Branch of the CAA. She is the 2002 literary award recipient of the Bernice Adams Cultural Awards for the City of Cambridge, and the 2006 winner of the Waterloo Regional Arts Council Award for best poetry. Becky is a member of the Cambridge Writers Collective, The Ontario Poetry Society, Pennsylvania State Poetry Society, and Green River Writers of Kentucky. She operates Craigleigh Press, a micro publishing company, which has published the works of over thirty deserving local writers.

By Becky D. Alexander: *More Tales from an Old Hespeler Girl* (2017), *Quern* (2013), *Growing Up in Hespeler* (2012), *Portals* (2009), *Shrapnel* (2009), *Translating Shadows* (2008), *haiku by two*

(2008), *Cloud Shine* (2006), *Sunshine Days* (2006), *Scratchings on the Moon* (2003), *Lost Boots* (2003), *In L.M.'s Garden* (2002), *Down Hammett's Lane* (2000), and *On Raven's Wings* (2000).

Donna Allard was raised in the fishing village of Richibucto, New Brunswick, which must surely lend its spice to her hardy spirit and well seasoned pen. Known to be able to "swear like a sailor," and "trot upon the earth shoeless," Allard's soulful eye captures the impact of light on the lens of a camera just as masterfully as she paints with words, often leaving one to feel like they should — "kiss a cod, grab a beer, have sex, and follow up with a cigarette" as stated in a review by Ronda Wicks. Donna has published four books of poetry. Donna owns and operates River Bones Press in New Brunswick. She served as the Canadian Poetry Association's *POEMATA* Newsletter Editor and on the CPA's Board of Directors as President from 2004-2012. She is a member of the Writers' Federation of New Brunswick. All Allard's books are based on her experience living in the Acadian culture. Allard's writing is described as "Purdyesque," by poet and publisher Chris Faiers, recipient of the Milton Acorn Memorial People's Poetry Award.

By Donna Allard: *From Shore to Shoormal* (Broken Jaw Press, 2013), *Minago Streets* (River Bones Press, 2006), *Bellwalker Devolution* (River Bones Press, 2006), and *Hand Upon the Dunes*, (River Bones Press, 2006).

Rosemary Aubert's poetry has been published in journals and anthologies over the nearly fifty years she has spent in Toronto after having immigrated from the United States. She has published four book-length collections.

By Rosemary Aubert: *Two Kinds of Honey, Picking Wild Raspberries, Lenin for Lovers*, and *Rough Wilderness*.

Henry Beissel started his career with the controversial political and literary journal *EDGE*, which he founded in Edmonton, Alberta, in 1963. Since then he has written and published around 40 books, including 22 collections of poetry, 6 books of plays, 10 books of translations of poetry and plays, and a book on Canada. His work has been translated into French, German, Chinese, Japanese, Polish, Turkish, and Hebrew. Patrick White wrote: "Henry Beissel is undoubtedly a Canadian poet of the first rank." The late F. R. Scott said about his *Cantos North*: "This epic is the first to see it [Canada and the North] in its entirety, as a matrix which binds the whole together in a national mythology." Beissel's play *Inook and the Sun* was premiered in Stratford in 1973. Beissel has taught medieval and modern English literature at Concordia University (Montreal) where he also founded a Creative Writing program that still flourishes today. He lives with his wife Arlette Francière, the literary translator and accomplished painter, in Ottawa, Ontario.

By Henry Beissel: POETRY: *What If Zen Gardens...*, with artwork by Arlette Francière (Toronto: Guernica Editions, 2017), *Cantos North / Cantos du Nord*, bilingual edition, French translation by Arlette Francière (Toronto: Guernica Editions, 2017), *Sightlines* (Toronto: Guernica Editions, 2016), *Fugitive Horizons / Flüchtigr Horizonte* bilingual edition, German translation by Heide Fruth-Sachs (Marburg, Germany: Verlag LiteraturWissenschaft, 2015), *Coming to Terms With a Child / Ein Kind Kommt Zur Sprache* (Marburg, Germany: Verlag LiteraturWissenschaft, 2015), *A Meteorology of Love* (Thornhill, Ontario: Beret Days Press, 2010), *Fugitive Horizons* (Toronto: Guernica Editions, 2013), *Coming to Terms With a Child* (Windsor, Ontario: Black Moss, 2011), *Across the Sun's Warp* (Ottawa: BuschekBooks, 2003), *The Dragon and the Pearl* (Ottawa: BuschekBooks, 2002), *Dying I Was Born* (Waterloo, Ontario: Penumbra Press, 1992), *Stones to Harvest* (Alexandria: Ayorama Editions, 1987) De luxe edition with woodcuts by Dale Alpen-Whiteside (Goderich, Ontario: Moonstone Press, 1993), *Ammonite* (Alexandria: Ayorama Editions, 1987), *Poems New and Selected* (Toronto: Mosaic Press, 1987), *Season of Blood* (Toronto: Mosaic Press, 1984), *Cantos North* (Alexandria: Ayorama Editions, 1980), *The Salt I Taste* (Montreal: DC Books, 1975), *Face On the Dark* (Toronto: New Press, 1970), *The World Is a Rainbow* (Toronto: Canadian Music Centre, 1968), *New Wings For Icarus* (Toronto: Coach House Press, 1966), and *Witness the Heart* (Toronto: Willow Green Press, 1963); PLAYS: *The Noose* (Winnipeg, 1985), *Under Coyote's Eye* (The Other Theatre, Chicago), *Improvisations For Mr X* (Montreal, 1978), *Goya* (Montreal, 1976), *For Crying Out Loud* (Toronto, 1975), *Inook and the Sun* (The Stratford Festival, 1973) and *Skinflint* (Montreal, 1969).

Nancy M. Bell is a proud Albertan and Canadian. She lives near Balzac, Alberta with her husband and various critters. She works with and fosters rescue animals. Nancy is a member of The Writers' Union of Canada and the Writers' Guild of Alberta. She has publishing credits in poetry, fiction, and non-fiction. For the past three years she has been invited to read her poetry at the Stephan G Stephansson House event Poetry at Stephan's House.

By Nancy M. Bell: FICTION: *His Brother's Bride, Landmark Roses* (writing as Marie Rafter), *On a Stormy Primeval Shore* (with Diane Scott Lewis), *Storm's Refuge, Come Hell or High Water, A Longview Wedding, A Longview Christmas, The Selkie's Song: Book 1 Arabella's Secret, Arabella Dreams: Book 2 Arabella's Secret, Henrietta's Heart* (with Pat Dale), *The Last Cowboy* (with Pat Dale), *She's Driving Me Crazy* (with Pat Dale), *The Teddy Dialogues, No Absolution, Laurel's Quest: Book 1 The Cornwall Adventures, A Step Beyond: Book 2 The Cornwall Adventures,* and *Go Gently: Book 3 The Cornwall Adventures*.

Sharon Berg writes poetry, stories, nonfiction, and book reviews, releasing books through Borealis Press (1979) and Coach House Press (1984). She also has several audio recordings: Gallery 101 (1985), Public Energies (1986), and Big Pond Rumours (2006). Then she took a hiatus for several years. Sharon founded and edits the international literary E-Zine *Big Pond Rumours*. She also edits and produces chapbooks for Canadian authors through her Micro Press, Big Pond Rumours. Her poetry and stories have appeared in periodicals or anthologies across Canada since the 1970s, such as: *Tamarack Review*, *Grain*, *Event*, *Poetry Canada Review*, and *The Fiddlehead*. Her work has also appeared in the USA, the UK, the Netherlands, and Australia. Recently, *The Name Unspoken: Wandering Spirit Survival School* was a chapter in *Alternative Schooling: Canadian Stories of Democracy within Bureaucracy*. She is currently working on arrangements for a book of poetry and release of a full-sized book about Wandering Spirit Survival School. She's also working on a novel and recently began to explore haiku as a fresh form for her poetry.

Steven Michael Berzensky (a.k.a. Mick Burrs) was born in California in 1940. After leaving the United States in 1965 to avoid the Vietnam War, he spent much of his life in Yorkton, Saskatchewan. While on the prairies, he edited *Grain* magazine, served as Yorkton's first writer-in-residence, and won the Saskatchewan Book Award for Poetry in 1998 for *Variations on the Birth of Jacob*. A comprehensive collection of his poetry, *The Names Leave the Stones: Poems New and Selected*, was published in 2001. Berzensky currently lives in Toronto, Ontario.

By Steven Michael Berzensky: *The Names Leave the Stones: Poems New and Selected* (Regina, Saskatchewan: Coteau Books, 2001), *Variations on the Birth of Jacob* (Winnipeg: The Muses' Company, 1997), *Dark Halo* (1993), *The Blue Pools of Paradise* (Regina, Saskatchewan: Coteau Books, 1983), *The Waking Image Bedside Companion* (1982), *Children on the Edge of Space* (Blue Mountain Books, 1977), *Moving in from Paradise* (Regina, Saskatchewan: Coteau Books, 1976), and *Game Farm: Poems for Intereflection 1967-1975* (1975).

Clara Blackwood is a poet and artist based in Toronto. She is the author of two poetry books, *Subway Medusa* (2007) and *Forecast* (2014), both with Guernica Editions. Her work has appeared in Canadian and international journals. She is a member of the League of Canadian Poets.

By Clara Blackwood: *Forecast* (Toronto: Guernica Editions, 2014), *Subway Medusa* (Toronto: Guernica Editions, 2007), *Love, virtually* (Toronto: Lyricalmyrical, 2006), *Visitations* (believe your own press, 2004), and *Under the Dragon's Tail* (believe your own press, 2002).

Robert A. Boates has been published in Tokyo, Lincoln, U.K., Houston, and Toronto. The poems in *Tamaracks* are from his fourth collection, *Man Without Memory: Poems New & Selected*. In 2009 he contributed poetry to the special Canadian issue of the British journal *Dream Catcher*.

Kent Bowman is the son of a professional trombonist who played with major U.S. dance bands and recording artists, Kent has developed his own musical skills as a trombonist, singer-guitarist, and songwriter. He worked professionally as a singer-guitarist and trombonist, playing with Celebration, Excelsior, and Flicks jazz bands, Edge of Dixie, Music Lovers swing band, and Upper Canada Brass Quintet. Currently, Kent plays and sings with the York Jazz Ensemble, a 9-piece swing band, playing music from classic jazz to swing. Kent has contributed poetry to such important anthologies as *Crossing Lines: Poets Who Came to Canada in the Vietnam War Era* (Seraphim Editions, 2008) and *And Left a Place to Stand On* (Hidden Brook Press, 2009).

By Kent Bowman: *On the Other Side of Paradise* (Brighton, Ontario: Hidden Brook Press), *Glasseaters' Banquet*, and *Purple Cowboy*.

Frances Boyle was born in Red Deer, Alberta and grew up in Winnipeg and Regina, all on the Canadian prairies. She is the author of a poetry collection, *Light-carved Passages* (BuschekBooks), a chapbook, *Portal Stones*, which won the Tree Press prize for chapbook manuscripts, and a novella, *Tower* (Fish Gotta Swim Editions). Her second collection of poetry, *This White Nest,* is forthcoming in 2019 from Quattro Books. As well, her poems and short fiction have appeared in literary magazines and anthologies throughout Canada and in the U.S., including most recently in *The Fiddlehead*, *The New Quarterly* and *The Antigonish Review*. She attended McGill University in Montreal, then lived for twelve years in Vancouver. Now well-settled in Ottawa, the nation's capital, she lives with her partner, Tim Stanley. They have two daughters, Elanor and Kasha. Frances is part of the editorial team at *Arc Poetry Magazine*. To learn more and to buy her books, visit her at www.francesboyle.com .

By Frances Boyle: POETRY: *Portal Stones* (Ottawa: Tree Press, 2014) and *Light-carved Passages* (Ottawa: BuschekBooks, 2014); FICTION: *Tower* (Amsterdam, The Netherlands: Fish Gotta Swim Editions, 2018).

Mary Lee Bragg lives in Ottawa. Her poetry and short fiction has been published in *Ascent*, *Grain*, the *Windsor Review*, *Queen's Quarterly*, and ezines in Canada and the US. She has published a novel (*Shooting Angels*, 2004) and two chapbooks of poetry, *How Women Work* and *Winter Music*.

By Mary Lee Bragg: *Winter Music* (Tree Press, 2013) and *How Women Work* (Grove Avenue Press, 2010).

Allan Briesmaster has been active on the Toronto-area literary scene since the 1980s as a workshop leader, reading series organizer, editor, and publisher. His work as an editor for Seraphim Editions in 2000-2008 culminated in the 76-poet anthology *Crossing Lines: Poets Who Came to Canada in the Vietnam War Era*. He was partner and editor in Quattro Books from 2006 to 2017. Since 2003 he has been publishing art and poetry chapbooks and full-length books with his own micro press, Aeolus House. Allan is the author of seven full-length books of poetry and eight shorter books. He has read his poetry, given talks, and hosted book launches at venues across Canada. In 2017 he was awarded Life Membership in The League of Canadian Poets. He lives in Thornhill, Ontario (just north of Toronto) with his wife Holly, a visual artist whose drawings, collages, and paintings have been reproduced in a number of his books and on some of their covers.

By Allan Briesmaster: *Pod and Berry* (Aeolus House, 2017), *River Neither* (Aeolus House, 2015), *Twenty-eight Sonnets* (Lyricalmyrical, 2014), *Against the Flight of Spring* (Quattro Books, 2013), *Confluences* (Seraphim Editions, 2009), *Temple of Fire* (Lyricalmyrical, 2008), *Interstellar* (Quattro Books, 2007), *The Other Seasons* (Hidden Brook Press, 2006), *Galactic Music* (Lyricalmyrical, 2005), *Pomona Summer* (Hidden Brook Press, 2004), *Urban-Pastoral* (Lyricalmyrical, 2004), *Phantelles* (Aeolus House, 2003), *Unleaving* (Hidden Brook Press, 2001), *The Tunnel Through the Trees* (Micro Prose, 1999), and *Weighted Light* (watershedBooks, 1998).

Ronnie R. Brown holds a B.A and M.A. from Concordia University (Montreal, Quebec) where she was the recipient of The Board of Governor's Medal and Graduate Poetry Prize. Brown has taught at both Concordia University and Carleton University (Ottawa, Ontario). The author of six full-length poetry collections and one chapbook, Brown has been published in magazines and anthologies in Canada, the U.S. and abroad. A staged adaptation of her work, *On Falling Bodies*, was presented at The Atelier of Ottawa's National Arts Centre. As well, Brown has produced/hosted a number of arts radio programs, most notably, SPARKS II (CHEZ-106 FM, Ottawa). Short-listed three times for the CBC Literary Awards, Brown's work has been recognized by numerous literary competitions, including: The Leacock Poetry Award, The Sandburg-Livesay Anthology Award (judge: Al Purdy), The *Canadian Stories* Poetry Competition, and The Golden Grassroots Chapbook Competition (judge: John B. Lee). Brown's collection, *States of Matter* (Black Moss Press, 2005), was awarded the Milton Acorn Memorial People's Poetry Award in 2006.

By Ronnie R. Brown: *Un-Deferred: A Draft dodger's Wife Remembers* (Bret Days, 2013), *Rocking on the Edge* (Black Moss Press, 2010), *Night Echoes* (Black Moss Press, 2006), *Photographic Evidence* (Black Moss Press, 2000), *Decisive Moments* (Anthos Books, 1988), and *Re Creation* (Balmuir Poetry Series, 1987).

April Bulmer's newest book *Out of Darkness, Light* will be released by Hidden Brook Press in 2018. She has many published books to her credit and her work has appeared in such celebrated

Canadian journals as *The Malahat Review, ARC,* and *PRISM international.* In the U.S., she has published in *The Anglican Theological Review* and *The Journal of Feminist Studies in Religion.* April holds Master's degrees in religious studies and theological studies, as well as creative writing. The poetry in this issue is an excerpt from her new manuscript "Buffalograss" which is set in a fictional town in Saskatchewan. April, however, was born and raised in Toronto but now lives in the small city of Cambridge, Ontario. Contact her at: april.poet@bell.net

Rebecca Clifford lives in Caledonia, Ontario (land of peace, harmony, and cheap cigarettes) with my husband, a bossy ginger cat, and a number of mutinous houseplants. Her poem "Dinah" appeared in the latest issue of *Tower* (January 2018). Her poem "Contemplotting" received a Judge's Choice award in The Ontario Poetry Society's Ultra Shorts competition, 2017. In 2017 she won 1st, 2nd & 3rd places in the Haldimand County Annual Poetry Contest. Her winning poems were 1: "Where the Lilies Grow", 2: "Coming Home", and 3: "Clearing Stones". Her poetry appears regularly in the *Niagara Anglican* newspaper. She has written poetry, prose, op eds, and tall tales for as long as she can remember. As Rebecca puts it, "I compose personalized poems for my quarrel of nieces and nephews, friends and family to mark the special occasions in their lives. Although the youngsters have outgrown the doggerel, they still read my stuff; now I inflict it on the general public with varying degrees of success. I'm not sure I've found my voice, but I'll keep 'singing' nonetheless."

Patrick Connors' chapbook, *Scarborough Songs*, was published by Lyricalmyrical in 2013, and charted on the Toronto Poetry Map. *Part-Time Contemplative*, his second chapbook with Lyricalmyrical, was released in 2016. He recently had work published in: *Canadian Stories* magazine, *di-vêrsé-city*, the anthology of the Austin International Poetry Festival, and the *Lummox 6* poetry anthology. This poem previously appeared in *Bottom of the Wine Jar*, one of 18 poems published by Sandcrab Press, and launched in Gibara, Cuba, in January of 2017. He is a manager for the Toronto chapter of 100,000 Poets for Change.

By Patrick Connors: *Part-Time Contemplative* (Toronto: Lyricalmyrical, 2016) and *Scarborough Songs* (Toronto: Lyricalmyrical, 2013).

Tony Cosier lives with his wife Janet in Ottawa, where he enjoyed teaching high school English for thirty years. He now writes full time and enjoys hiking and canoeing the Rideau River trails and waterways. Tony is the author of eight volumes of poetry, two poetry chapbooks, six plays, a novel, and a book of short stories. His poetry has been widely published in anthologies and literary magazines internationally. He has won the Tree Theatre National Playwrights Prize and the General Store Publishing House National Short Story Contest. Tony has been shortlisted three times for the Ottawa Book Award, and was a finalist for the Lampman Award four times. Three poems by Tony were recently nominated by *The Prairie Journal* for the 2018 Canadian National Magazine Awards. He is currently working on *Natural Magic,* a collection of poems.

By Tony Cosier: *Carillonneur* (Penumbra Press, 2012), *The Spirit Dances* (Penumbra Press, 2005), *Clearwater Tarn* (Penumbra Press, 1999), *Kilmarnock* (Penumbra Press, 1994), *Landsinger* (Penumbra Press, 1989), *In the Face of the Storm* (Anthos Books, 1987), *Cubist Ghazals* (Cannon Press, 1986), and *My Youth* (Vesta Publications, 1983).

Lorna Crozier has received the Governor General's Award, three Pat Lowther Awards, the 2011 Kloeppenburg Award for Literary Excellence, and five honourary doctorates, most recently from McGill and Simon Fraser. In 2013 she received B.C.'s Lieutenant's Governor's Lifetime Achievement Award. A Fellow of the Royal Society of Canada and an Officer of the Order of Canada, she has published 18 books of poetry, the latest two called *What the Soul Doesn't Want* and *The Wrong Cat.* Her memoir, *Small Beneath the Sky,* was included on Amazon's list of the 100 books one should read in a lifetime, and *The Book of Marvels: A Compendium of Everyday Things* was one of *The Globe and Mail's* top 100 books of 2012. Her poems have been translated into several languages, including a book-length translation in French and another in Spanish, and she has read in every continent, except Antarctica. A Professor Emerita at the University of Victoria, she lives on Vancouver Island with Patrick Lane, two turtles, many fish and two fine cats.

By Lorna Crozier: POETRY: *What the Soul Doesn't Want* (2017), *The Wrong Cat* (2015), *The Blue Hour of the Day: Selected Poems* (2007), *Whetstone* (2005), *Bones in Their Wings: Ghazals* (2003), *Apocrypha of Light* (2002), *What the Living Won't Let Go* (1999), *A Saving Grace* (1996), *Everything Arrives at the Light* (1995), *Inventing the Hawk* (1992), *Angels of Flesh, Angels of Silence* (1988), *The Garden Going On Without Us* (1985), *The Weather* (1983), *No Longer Two People* (with Patrick Lane, 1981), *Humans and Other Beasts* (1980), *Crow's Black Joy* (1979), and *Inside Is the Sky* (1976); NON-FICTION: *The Book of Marvels: A Compendium of Everyday Things* (2012) and *Small Beneath the Sky* (2009).

Phillip Crymble received his MFA from the University of Michigan and now lives in Fredericton, New Brunswick, where he is a SSHRC doctoral fellow in the English Department at the University of New Brunswick. A poetry editor at *The Fiddlehead* since 2012, his poems have appeared in *The New York Quarterly, Michigan Quarterly Review, Tar River Poetry, The Hollins Critic, The Literary Review of Canada, Poetry Ireland Review, The Salt Anthology of New Writing 2013, Oxford Poetry, The Forward Book of Poetry 2017,* and elsewhere. In 2016, *Not Even Laughter,* his first full-length collection, was a finalist for both the New Brunswick Book Award and the Writer's Federation of Nova Scotia's J.M. Abraham Prize.

By Phillip Crymble: *Not Even Laughter* (Knockeven, Cliffs of Moher, County Clare, Ireland: Salmon Poetry, 2015) and *Wide Boy* (Belfast, Northern Ireland: Lapwing Publications, 2007).

Robert Currie is a founding board member of the Saskatchewan Festival of Words and a former chairman of the Saskatchewan Writers' Guild. Currie once edited and published *Salt*, a little magazine of contemporary writing. Highlights of his career include teaching creative writing at the Saskatchewan School of the Arts in Fort San and the Sage Hill Writing Experience in Lumsden, delivering the Anne Szumigalsaki Memorial Lecture for the League of Canadian poets, and serving two terms as Saskatchewan Poet Laureate. Currie is a recipient of the Saskatchewan Lieutenant Governor's Award for Lifetime Achievement in the Arts. His next collection, *One-Way Ticket*, will be published in fall, 2018.

By Robert Currie: POETRY: *The Days Run Away* (Coteau, 2015), *Witness* (Hagios, 2009), *Running in Darkness* (Coteau, 2006), *Klondike Fever* (Coteau, 1992), *Learning On the Job* (Oberon, 1986), *Yarrow* (Oberon 1980), *Diving Into Fire* (Oberon, 1977), *Moving Out* (Coteau, 1975), *The Halls of Elsinore* (Sesame Press, 1973), *Sawdust and Dirt* (Fiddlehead Poetry Books, 1973), and *Quarterback #1* (Delta, 1970); FICTION: *Living With the Hawk* (Thistledown, 2013), *Teaching Mr. Cutler* (Coteau, 2002), *Things You Don't Forget* (Coteau, 1999), and *Night Games* (Coteau, 1983).

David Day is a poet and author of fifty books of poetry, history, fantasy, ecology, natural history, mythology, and fiction. Day's books — for both adults and children — have sold over three million copies worldwide and have been translated into twenty languages. www.daviddaybooks.com

By David Day: POETRY: *Nevermore: A Book of Hours* (Toronto: Quattro Books, 2012), *Just Say 'No' to Family Values* (Exile Editions, 1997), *Visions and Prophecies of St Louis the Metis* (Thistledown Press,1997), *Aska's Sea Creatures* (Toronto: Doubleday, 1994), *Aska's Birds* (Toronto: Doubleday, 1992), *Aska's Animals* (Toronto: Doubleday, 1991), *Gothic* (Exile Editions, 1986), *The Animals Within* (Penumbra Press, 1984), *The Scarlet Coat Serial* (Press Porcepic, 1981), and *The Cowichan* (Oolichan, 1975); TOLKIEN FANTASY: *The Dark Powers of Tolkien* (Octopus-Bounty, 2018), *The Heroes of Tolkien* (Octopus-Bounty, 2017), *The Battles of Tolkien* (Octopus-Bounty, 2016), *Tolkien: An Illustrated Atlas* (Octopus-Bounty, 2015), *Tolkien: A Dictionary* (Octopus-Bounty, 2013), *The World of Tolkien: Mythological Sources of Lord of the Rings* (Octopus-Bounty, 2002), *The Hobbit Companion* (Pavilion Books, 1997), *Tolkien's Ring* (Harper-Collins, 1994), *A to Z of Tolkien* (Mandarin, 1993), *Tolkien: The Illustrated Encyclopedia* (Michael Beazley, 1992), and *A Tolkien Bestiary* (Michael Beazley, 1979); CHILDREN'S BOOKS: *King of the Woods* (Andersen Press, 1993), *Tippu* (Piccadilly Press, 1993), *The Wolf Children* (Piccadilly Press, 1991), *The Big Lie* (Piccadilly Press, 1991), *The Sleeper* (Piccadilly Press, 1990), *The Swan Children* (Piccadilly Press, 1989), and *The Emperor's Panda* (Toronto: McClelland & Stewart, 1986); ECOLOGY/

NATURAL HISTORY: *The Complete Rhinoceros* (EIA Books, 1994), *Green Penguin Children's Book Guide* (Penguin Books, 1992), *True Tales of Environmental Madness* (Pelham, 1990), *Noah's Choice* (Viking-Penguin, 1990), *The Encyclopedia of Vanished Species* (Universal Books, 1989), *The Eco Wars* (Harper-Collins, 1989), *The Whale War* (Routledge, 1987), and *The Doomsday Book of Animals* (Ebury Press, 1981); OTHER: *Alice'a Adventures in Wonderland Decoded* (Penguin, 2015), *The Quest for King Arthur* (De Agostini, 1996), *Castles* (Bantam, 1984), and *The Burroughs Bestiary* (New English Library, 1978).

James Deahl was born in Pittsburgh in 1945, and grew up in that city as well as in the Laurel Highlands region of the Appalachian Mountains. He is the author of twenty-seven literary titles, the most recent being *Red Haws To Light The Field* and *To Be With A Woman*. A cycle of his poems is the focus of a one-hour TV special, *Under the Watchful Eye* (Silver Falls Video Productions, 1993). The audiotape of *Under the Watchful Eye* was released by Broken Jaw Press in 1995. (These have been reissued on CD and DVD by Silver Falls.) Since 1970 he has made his home in Canada, where he writes, edits, and translates full-time. He currently resides in Sarnia and is a member of After Hours Poets. Deahl is the father of Sarah, Simone, and Shona, with whom he is translating the poetry of the Québécois poet Émile Nelligan into English.

By James Deahl: POETRY: *Red Haws To Light The Field* (Toronto: Guernica Editions, 2017), *To Be With A Woman* (San Pedro, California: Lummox Press, 2016), *Landscapes*, with Katherine L. Gordon (Metulla, Israel: Cyclamens and Swords, 2016), *Unbroken Lines* (San Pedro, California: Lummox Press, 2015), *Two Paths Through The Seasons*, with Norma West Linder (Metulla, Israel: Cyclamens and Swords, 2014), *North Point* (Toronto: Lyricalmyrical, 2012), *Rooms The Wind Makes* (Toronto: Guernica Editions, 2012), *North Of Belleville* (Brighton, Ontario: Hidden Brook Press, 2012), *Opening The Stone Heart* (Thornhill, Ontario: Aeolus House, 2010), *No Star Is Lost* (Toronto: Lyricalmyrical, 2009), *Love Where Our Nights Are Long* (Mt. Pleasant, Ontario: Laurel Reed Books, 2008), *If Ever Two Were One* (Thornhill, Ontario: Aeolus House, 2008), *When Rivers Speak* (Pittsburgh: Unfinished Monument Press, 2001), *Blackbirds* (Hamilton, Ontario: Unfinished Monument Press, 1999), *Tasting The Winter Grapes* (Newport, Dyfed, Wales: Envoi Poets Publications, 1995), *Even This Land Was Born Of Light* (Goderich, Ontario: Moonstone Press, 1993), *Heartland* (Newport, Dyfed, Wales: Envoi Poets Publications, 1993), *Geschriebene Bilder* (Berlin, Germany: M+N Boesche Verlag, 1990), *A Stand Of Jackpine*, with Milton Acorn (Toronto: Unfinished Monument Press, 1987), *Into This Dark Earth*, with Raymond Souster (Toronto: Unfinished Monument Press, 1985), *Blue Ridge* (Willowdale, Ontario: Aureole Point Press, 1985), *No Cold Ash* (Victoria, British Columbia: Sono Nis Press, 1984), *Steel Valley* (Willowdale, Ontario: Aureole Point Press, 1984), and *In The Lost Horn's Call* (Willowdale, Ontario: Aureole Point Press, 1982); PROSE: *Real Poetry* (Toronto: Unfinished Monument Press, 1981); MEMOIR/POETRY: *Under The Watchful Eye* (Fredericton, New Brunswick: Broken Jaw Press, 1995) TRANSLATION: *The River's Stone Roots: Two dozen poems by Tu Fu* (Mississauga, Ontario: Serengeti Press, 2005).

Stewart Donovan was born in Ingonish, Cape Breton, Nova Scotia. He studied Modern Literature at St. Francis Xavier University where he received his B.A. He received an M.A. from the University of Ottawa, and his Ph.D. in Anglo-Irish Literature and Drama from University College Dublin. For the past 33 years Donovan has taught Modern literature, drama, film, and cultural studies at St. Thomas University. Professor Donovan is the founder of the university's Irish Studies Program, its Film and Media Program, and of *The Nashwaak Review*, a literary, arts, history and cultural magazine. His biography of R. J. MacSween, *The Forgotten World*, was short listed for both of Atlantic Canada's non-fiction awards. He has published three volumes of poetry and his second novel, *Wake of the Aspy* came out in 2013. He's completing a book on cultural and political identity, *Ingonish to Inishowen: A Wayward Irish Identity*, and a collection of poems on the First World War, *In the Shadow of Vimy*. He is a member of CAIS and the International Ezra Pound Society. For further information: http://w3.stu.ca/stu//sites/nble/d/donovan_stewart_leo.htmlhttp://w3.stu.ca/stu/academic/departments/english_lit/faculty/donovan/index.aspx http://thechronicleherald.ca/books/1124187-a-view-from-north-of-smokey

By Stewart Donovan: POETRY: *In the Shadow of Vimy: Poems on World War 1 and other subjects* (Breton Books, 2018), *Wake of the Aspy* (Breton Books 2013), *Ingonish Out: New and Selected Poems* (Breton Books, 2011), *The Molly Poems and Highland Elegies* (Breton Books, 2005), and *Cape Breton Quarry* (Breton Books, 1992); PROSE: *The Forgotten World: a life of R.J. MacSween* (Cape Breton University Press, 2007) and *Maritime Union: A Political Tale* (Non-Entity Press, 1992).

G. W. Down is a poet, lyricist, editor, and business consultant who lives in Hamilton, Ontario. He is also a partner in The Book Band, a company which does marketing, distribution and promotion for Canadian publishers.

By G. W. Down: *Down For The Count* (Manor House Publishing, 2002) and *For Your Any Mood* (Vantage Press, 1976).

Gertrude (Trudi) Olga Down has been writing and reading poetry since she was a young child. She began to write with more commitment after joining The Tower Poetry Society in the 1980s. Typically using the free verse style, Trudi's poetry offers personal insights on the human condition, and on nature and love. She strives to present these word pictures in poetry that is accessible to all readers.

Jennifer Lynn Dunlop has been writing poetry for as long as she can remember. She has numerous poems published in such places as *The Queen's Feminist Review*, the anthology *Scaling the Face of Reason*, as well as *Tower Poetry* books and *The Banister*.

Bernadette Gabay Dyer is a published novelist, short story writer, poet, and playwright. She is also a Storyteller who works for Toronto Public Libraries. Her work has been included in anthologies such as *Bite to Eat Place*. Her short stories have been published in literary journals that include *Wasafiri* from St Mary's College University of London England, *The Toronto South Asian Review*, and *Kola Magazine* from Montreal, etc. Her poetry was first published in chapbooks from Plowman Press, titled *Of the Earth and From the Sky*, and also *Lena by the Lake*. Her novels are: *Waltzes I Have not Forgotten*, as well as, *Abductors*. Her short story collection is *Villa Fair*. Bernadette runs an Open Mic program in conjunction with the library she works at in Toronto, to encourage and give exposure to the work of writers of all genres.

By Bernadette Gabay Dyer: POETRY: *Of the Earth and From the Sky* and *Lena by the Lake*; FICTION: *Waltzes I Have not Forgotten*, *Abductors*, and *Villa Fair*.

Margaret Patricia Eaton is a poet and freelance writer in Moncton, New Brunswick. After surviving a 32-year career in education, she embarked on her dream career. Since 2006 she's published three poetry collections and had work selected for several anthologies including *Voices, voices, voices: A second decade of poems from Voices Israel* (2010), *Under the Mulberry Tree: Poems for & about Raymond Souster* (Toronto: Quattro Books, 2013), and *150: Canada's History in Poetry* (Charlottetown, PEI: Acorn Press, 2018). Her poem "Celtic Trilogy" won First Place in the 2009 Writers' Federation of New Brunswick Creative Writing Competition (Single poem category) and her piece, "Ruminations on Rumi" won Third Place in the 2018 competition (Creative non-fiction category). She's written over 1,000 articles for a variety of magazines and newspapers and for seven years wrote "Art Talk," a weekly arts review column for the Moncton *Times & Transcript*. She's a graduate of Mount Allison University (B.A.; B. Ed.) and the University of New Brunswick (M. Ed.). Member: Writers' Federation of New Brunswick; Professional Writers Association of Canada.

By Margaret Patricia Eaton: POETRY: *Vision & Voice,* with paintings by Angelica De Benedetti (2011), *Painted Poems,* with paintings by Angelica De Benedetti (2008), and *Seeking Grace,* with memories by Victoria Beasley Eaton (2006), all three from Eagle Wings Press, Moncton, New Brunswick; NON-FICTION: *Fundy: Hidden Jewel of the North Atlantic,* edited and co-authored with R. J. Cunningham (Dorchester, New Brunswick: Westmorland Historical Society, 2010).

Ronda Wicks Eller was born in Toronto and raised in Woodstock, Ontario. She released her first chapbook in 1995 and now has three 60-80 page books in print with a fourth one in progress. Ronda's work is published in Canada, U.S.A., England, and Bangladesh in various literary journals and anthologies. She has received awards, facilitated poetry workshops,

adjudicated competitions, and reviewed others' work. As the owner of Sky-Wing Press, she functions as editor, artist, layout designer, and publisher. She was Media Coordinator on the Canadian Poetry Association's Board of Directors 2004-2012 and is Consul for the Canadian Poetry Guild (its rebranded name) since 2016, and also co-administrator of its Facebook groups since 2012. Ronda was an Associate Member of the League of Canadian Poets from 2008-2009. Her website is http://rwicksellercwg.wix.com/home .
She is also on Facebook: https://www.facebook.com/pages/Canadian-Poet-Ronda-Eller/147211261965546?fref=ts, on Youtube: http://www.youtube.com/channel/UCCeDyKvYXw9JCp_HEMwcNNw and on Twitter @RWicksEller

By Ronda Wicks Eller: *The Lion and the Golden Calf* (Sky-Wing Press, 2008), *Whale Songs in the Aurora Borealis* (HMS Press, 2005), and *My Harmonic Perfection* (HMS Press and Atlantic Disk Publishers, 1995).

Daniela Elza's work has appeared nationally and internationally in over 100 publications. Her poetry collections are *the weight of dew* (Mother Tongue Publishing, 2012), *the book of It* (iCrow Publications, 2011), and most recently *milk tooth bane bone* (Leaf Press, 2013), of which David Abram says: "Out of the ache of the present moment, Daniela Elza has crafted something spare and irresistible, an open armature for wonder." Daniela earned her doctorate in Philosophy of Education from Simon Fraser University (2011) and has continued to contribute to Poetic Inquiry. In the literary community Daniela guest-edits for journals/anthologies, judges contests, organizes and promotes events, collaborates with other artists, performs and conducts workshops. She also helps coordinate and host Twisted Poets reading series. She lives and writes in Vancouver, British Columbia. For more information visit: http://strangeplaces.livingcode.org/

By Daniela Elza: *milk tooth bane bone* (Leaf Press, 2013), *the weight of dew* (Mother Tongue Publishing, 2012), and *the book of It* (iCrow Publications, 2011).

Joseph A. Farina is a retired lawyer who has been writing poetry since he was thirteen. He is the author of two books of poetry, *The Cancer Chronicles*, and *The Ghosts of Water Street*, both from Serengeti Press. He has been published in many poetry anthologies throughout Canada, the USA, and Europe and has received awards from *Philadelphia Poets* and the City of Sarnia, where he lives. He has been in the last three Lummox Press anthologies and is currently working on a book about growing up as a Sicilian immigrant teenager in love with those who owned the tracks.

By Joseph A. Farina: *The Cancer Chronicles* and *The Ghosts of Water Street* (both from Serengeti Press).

Venera Fazio (1946-2017) was born in Bafia, Sicily, and at the age of five she migrated to Dundas, Ontario, Canada with her family. After retiring as a social worker, to raise her children, her passion for literature led her to becoming a writer. She joined the Association of Italian Canadian Writers, taking on several executive roles, including that of President and organizer of national conferences. Known as a champion and supporter of other writers, Venera co-edited ten literary anthologies, which featured writers from North America, Italy, and Australia. One of the highlights for her as editor was the publication *of Sweet Lemons: Writings with a Sicilian Accent* in 2004 and the follow up *of Sweet Lemons 2* in 2010 — these publications highlighted Venera's Sicilian heritage, of which she was very proud. Over the years, her stories and poems were featured in several literary magazines and anthologies; in 2016, she published her collection of poetry, *The Fabric of My Soul*. Venera was passionate about her work and proud of her achievements as writer, poet, and literary editor.

By Venera Fazio: *The Fabric of My Soul* (Montreal: Longbridge Books, 2015).

Fran Figge is currently president of The Ontario Poetry Society, Past President of Hamilton's Tower Poetry Society, and a member of the Canadian Authors Association. She has read poetry and won contests across Ontario and west to Vancouver. *fall float fly* is a selection of many of her prize-winning poems. Fran also has a chapbook entitled *hope and despair in the ark*, and *Encompass II* features her work and four other poets. She has helped judge poetry contests, edited and compiled *The PoeTrain Anthology A Selection of Train Poems by Canadian Poets*, The *Encompass Series Poetry Anthologies III and V* and the *Scarlet Thistles Anthology of Canadian Poets*. The escarpment in Stoney Creek, Ontario is her calming breath, her backyard refuge, and her inspiration.

By Fran Figge: *fall float fly* (Thornhill, Ontario: Beret Days Press, 2016) and
hope and despair in the ark (Toronto: Lyricalmyrical, 2013).

Doris Fiszer is an Ottawa poet whose poems have appeared in a variety of publications including *Bywords Quarterly Journal*, bywords.ca and the *Voice*. She has a poem in the anthology *When All Else Fails: Motherhood in Precarious Times*, (Demeter Press). Her chapbook, *The Binders,* was the 2016 winner of Tree Press's chapbook contest. Her poem, "Zen Garden," won the 2017 John Newlove Poetry Award. As the recipient of this award, she has been offered the opportunity to publish a chapbook in 2018 through Bywords. *The Binders* was also shortlisted for the 2017 bpNichol Chapbook Award. As well, she is an associate member of The League of Canadian Poets. Doris has recently completed a full-length poetry collection and is currently writing poems about her mother.

By Doris Fiszer: *The Binders* (Tree Press, 2016).

Kate Marshall Flaherty is presently the writer in residence at The Heliconian Club in Toronto. She is the Toronto representative for the League of Canadian Poets, and founder of the Canadian version of the "Poet is in: valentines and railway lines in union," station, emulating past New York Poet Laureate Marie Howe's initiative of bringing poetry to Travellers across borders. Kate guides Stillpoint writing workshops, is an in-house editor for Quattro Books, and head of Quattro Books' "best new poets in Canada" contest and publications series. She lives in teaches in Toronto. Poetry is her lifeline.

By Kate Marshall Flaherty: POETRY: *Stone Soup* (Toronto: Quattro Books, 2015), *Reaching V* (Toronto: Guernica Editions, 2014), *where we are going* (Piquant Press, 2012), *Tilted Equilibrium* (Brighton, Ontario: Hidden Brook Press, 2008) and *String of Mysteries* (Brighton, Ontario: Hidden Brook Press, 2006); PLAY: *Why Not the Moon* (Great Canadian Theatre Co., 1991).

Jennifer L. Foster's poems have appeared in the *Lummox* and *Cats, Cats, Cats, and More Cats* (Mini Mocho Press) anthologies as well as *Quills Canadian Poetry Magazine* and *Tower Poetry*. Her short stories have been published in *Perspectives Magazine* (online). Jennifer enjoys writing for both adults and children. She is a graduate of Queen's University (Kingston, Ontario) with an Honours B.A. in English and a B.Ed. Jennifer lives in Hamilton, Ontario.

Linda Frank was born in Montreal but now lives in Hamilton, Ontario. She has three books of poetry with a fourth due out in the Spring of 2018. Her second book, *Kahlo: The World Split Open*, was shortlisted for the Pat Lowther Poetry Prize in 2009. Linda won the Bliss Carmen Poetry Prize in 2008, was nominated for a national Magazine Award in 2009, and was a finalist for the National Magazine Award in 2014. She has been a finalist in several contests including most recently *Malahat*'s Open Season Award. She's a past winner of a Hamilton and Region Arts Council Literary Award for Short Work, Poetry. She has been shortlisted for *Arc's* Poem of the Year, *Fiddlehead's* Ralph Gustafson Award, *This Magazine*'s Great Canadian Literary Hunt, the Sandburg-Livesay Anthology Contest, the Acorn-Rukeyser Chapbook Award, and contests sponsored by *Contemporary Verse 2*. Her website is lindafrank.ca

By Linda Frank: *Divided* (Hamilton, Ontario: Wolsak and Wynn, 2018), *Insomnie Blues* (Ottawa: BuschekBooks, 2011), *Kahlo: The World Split* (Ottawa: BuschekBooks, 2008), *Cobalt Moon Embrace* (Ottawa: BuschekBooks, 2002), *Taste the Silence* (Flying Turtle Press, 1996), *...It Takes A Train To Cry* (SolitaryBird Press, 1998), and *Orpheus Descending* (SolitaryBirdPress, 1998).

Ryan Gibbs lives in London, Ontario, and is pursuing a Ph.D. at the University of Western Ontario. He is an English professor and coordinator at Lambton College in nearby Sarnia, where he is also a member of After Hours Poets, and has read his poetry in the City Council as part of the nation-wide Mayor's Poetry City Challenge. He is also a member of The League of Canadian Poets. His poems have appeared in *Tower Poetry, The Windsor Review*, *Under the Mulberry Tree*, and *Whisky Sour City*. His children's poetry has been included in the State of Texas Assessment of Academic Readiness.

Sharon Goodier is a poet from Toronto. She has been published in U.S. in *Adana Women's Spirituality Anthology*, *Tin Lunchbox*, *Terrene*, *Persimmon Tree*, *Lost Sparrow Porcupine Anthology*, *Poets Reading the News*. Her short story "The Year of the Donkey" was published by *New Legends Anthology*. In Canada she has been published in *Carte Blanche* and *Quilliad*. Her chapbook *Primal Elegies* was published by Missing Link Press (Toronto). She self-published a chapbook of social justice poetry *A Stone in My Shoe*, is a co-founder of the renewed Art Bar Reading Series, an instigator of the Engaged Poetry Meet Up, and an annual host of 100,000 Poets for Change.

By Sharon Goodier: *A Stone in My Shoe* (self-published, 2016) and *Primal Elegies* (Toronto: Missing Link Press, 1975).

Katherine L. Gordon is a rural Ontario poet, publisher, essayist, judge, editor, and reviewer, working to promote the flowering of Canadian literature in this exciting era when Canadian writers are recognized as amongst the best in the world. She enjoys working with fine contemporaries in collaborations, chapbooks, and anthologies. Her work has often been translated and is archived in Canadian universities. Her latest anthology publication is *Piping at the End-of-Days: A book of Overcoming* (Rockwood, Ontario: Valley Press, 2017).

By Katherine L. Gordon: *Translating Shadows* (Cambridge, Ontario: Craigleigh Press), *All Here Sail in a River of Light* (Harmonia Press), *Light Rescue* (Melinda Cochrane International Press), *Landscapes*, with James Deahl (Metulla, Israel: Cyclamens and Swords Publishing), *What Lightning Brings* (Metulla, Israel: Cyclamens and Swords Publishing), *In Moonlight the Sky Will Slide* (Metulla, Israel: Cyclamens and Swords Publishing), *Telling Lies* (Metulla, Israel: Cyclamens and Swords Publishing), *After the River Freezes* (PATC Press), *Creative Chaos* (PATC Press), *Coast Lines*, and *An Impact of Butterflies*.

Elizabeth Greene was born in New York City and came to Canada in 1965 to do graduate work in Medieval Studies and English at the University of Toronto. During her graduate work, she gathered a group which started a literary magazine, *Catalyst*. Contributors included Margaret Atwood, Margaret Avison, Gary Geddes, Dennis Lee, and Rafael Barreto-Rivera (later of the Four Horsemen). After completing her Ph.D., she began teaching at Queen's University in Kingston, Ontario, where she was a founder of Women's Studies and was instrumental in introducing Creative Writing to her department and the university. She has studied writing with Sharon Olds, Barry Dempster, and Helen Humphreys, and holds a certificate in Creative Writing from Humber College. She has published poetry, short fiction, and essays in journals and anthologies. She lives in Kingston, Ontario, with her son and two cats.

By Elizabeth Greene: *A Season Among Psychics* (Inanna, 2018), *Understories* (Inanna, 2014), *Moving* (Inanna, 2010), *The Iron Shoes* (Brighton, Ontario: Hidden Brook Press, 2007), and *The Moon Card,* (Star Press, 2001).

Andreas Gripp is the author of 23 books of poetry, 16 chapbooks, and 3 books of fiction. Poems by Andreas Gripp have most recently appeared in the anthologies *Piping at the End-of-Days* (Valley Press, 2017), *Another London* (Harmonia Press, 2016), *Moon Shine: A Canadian Poetry Collection* (Craigleigh Press, 2015), *Window Fishing: The night we caught Beatlemania* (Hidden Brook Press, 2014), and *Under The Mulberry Tree: Poems For & About Raymond Souster* (Quattro Books, 2014). His book *Anathema* was shortlisted for the Acorn-Plantos Award for Peoples' Poetry in 2010. His latest book of poems is *Panthera Leo* (Harmonia Press, 2017). He presently lives in London, Ontario, with his wife Carrie Lee, and their two cats, Mabel and Mila

By Andreas Gripp: POETRY: *Panthera Leo and other poems* (2017), *Seasonal Psalms* (2017), *Selected Poems 2000-2016* (2016), *Christmas Poems* (2016), *Apocrypha: Poems Selected & New Volume 3* (2015), *Holy Rollers* (2015), *The Better Kiss* (2014), *All Here Sail in a River of Light* (2014), *The Rest of Yesterday* (2014), *The Penitent, or Cannon Foster's Dissonance Revolution* (2013), *The Breakfast of Birds* (2013), *Selected Poems 2000-2012* (2013), *The Apostasy of Daylight* (2012), *Garden Sunrise* (2012), *Perennial: Poems Selected & New Volume 2* (2011), *Ex gratia* (2011), *Under the Evergreens* (2011), *The Fall* (2010), *Metronome* (2010), *In the Breath of Woven Seasons* (Haiku) (2010), *Anathema: Poems Selected & New* (2009), *The Lesser Light* (2009), *Dr. Lerner's Study Notes* (2009), *Beads on Blossoms* (2008), *Angel Clare* (2007), *T.O. Loveless & other poems* (2007), *In a Sea of Green Tea* (Shan-zi) (2007), *The Language of Sparrows* (2006), *Past Life Aggression & other poems* (2006), *Like Darwin Among the Gods* (2005), *Anno Domino* (Haiku/Senryu) (2005), *Mr. Rubik's House of Cards* (2004), *The After Solstice* (2004), *The Cosmopolitan Day of Reckoning* (2003), *Captain Fascist and the Plastic Storm Troopers* (2002), *Gullible Skeptic* (2001), *Captain Fascist* (2001), *Fish Out of Water* (2000), and *Deceived* (1999); FICTION: *Day Dreams* (2016), *Reich of the Amazon* (1993), and *Cairo's Power* (1992).

Richard M. Grove, otherwise known to friends as Tai, divides his time between a condo in Toronto and a house in Brighton. The Brighton house is in Presqu'ile Provincial Park, ½ way between Toronto and Kingston where he and his wife, Kim, run a B&B. He is a poet, prose writer, publisher, photographer, painter, graphic designer, and is the founding president of the CCLA - Canada Cuba Literary Alliance. You can find his Cuba Blog at: http://cubablog.hiddenbrookpress.com/. His many titles of poetry, prose, and memoir can be found on Amazon. He has fourteen titles to his name and his images have been used in many books as well as on the cover of almost seventy-five books. His writer's blog is – https://richardgrovewriter.wordpress.com/. He has had over 100 poems and essays published in periodicals around the world as well as having been published in over 30 anthologies. He publishes an art and literature magazine called *Devour: Art & Lit Canada*. Find Hidden Brook Press at www.HiddenBrookPress.com.

David Haskins is the author of *This House Is Condemned* (Wolsak & Wynn), a literary memoir, and *Reclamation* (Borealis), poetry. His writing appears in over 30 literary journals *(Lummox, The Oxfordian, Windsor Review, Fiddlehead, Prism, Journal of Canadian Fiction)*, anthologies and books. His work has been broadcast coast to coast. Earlier writings include reviews as a theatre critic for *Onion*, a Toronto Arts paper. He has won first prizes from the CBC, the Canadian Authors Association, the Ontario Poetry Society, and three times from Arts Hamilton. In 1953, Haskins emigrated from England to Beamsville, Ontario, at the age of eight. He now lives in neighbouring Grimsby. His secondary school teaching spans 35 years, five as Department Head of English. He also mentored graduate students at Brock University's College of Education, and wrote and taught courses in creative writing and journalism for Ontario's Ministry of Education. He is currently working on a poetry book, a chapbook, and a young adult fantasy novel, or out cruising country roads in his 1970 MGB.

By David Haskins: *This House Is Condemned* (Hamilton, Ontario: Wolsak & Wynn, 2013) and *Reclamation* (Borealis Press, 1980).

Rhoda Hassmann has been a resident of Hamilton, Ontario since 1976. After a career of 41 years as a university professor specializing in international human rights, she retired in 2016. Many of her poems reflect stories she has encountered in her research or in person about violations of people's human rights. She has published in various local anthologies. In 2014 she published two poems, "Re-Asssessment" and "Reading about Cannibalism" in *Arborealis*: *A Canadian Anthology of Poetry* (ed. K.V. Skene). In 2017 her poem, "Grave Marker" received an honorable mention in *The Banister: Niagara Poetry Anthology,* (vol. 32). Her study, *Compassionate Canadians*, was named 2004 Outstanding Book in Human Rights by the Human Rights Section, American Political Science Association; her *Economic Rights in Canada and the United States* was named a notable book for 2008 by the United States Human Rights Network. She also served as a Senior Editor of the *Encyclopedia of Human Rights* (2010), and has published numerous articles and book chapters on various aspects of international and Canadian human rights.

By Rhoda Hassmann: NON-FICTION: *In Defense of Universal Human Rights* (Polity Press, 2018), *State Food Crimes* (Cambridge University Press, 2016), *Can Globalization Promote Human Rights?* (Penn State University Press, 2010), *Reparations to Africa* (University of Pennsylvania Press, 2008), *Compassionate Canadians: Civic Leaders Discuss Human Rights* (2003), *Human Rights and the Search for Community* (1995), *Human Rights in Commonwealth Africa* (1986), and *Colonialism and Underdevelopment in Ghana* (1978).

Debbie Okun Hill is a Canadian poet who gardens words full-time in rural southwestern Ontario. She is a member of The League of Canadian Poets and the Writers' Union of Canada, and is a former President of The Ontario Poetry Society and a former co-host of Sarnia's Spoken Word event. To date, over 380 of her poems have been published in publications/e-zines including *Blast Furnace, Lummox, Mobius, Still Point Arts Quarterly, The Binnacle, THEMA,* and *Phati'tude Literary Magazine* in the United States plus *Descant, Existere, Other Voices, The Literary Review of Canada,* and *Vallum* in Canada. She has four chapbooks: *Swaddled in Comet Dust, Another Trail of Comet Dust, Drawing from Experience,* and *Chalk Dust Clouds,* winner of TOPS Golden Grassroots Poetry Award. *Tarnished Trophies* is her first trade book. Her next book focuses on the ash trees destroyed by the emerald ash borer. She blogs about literary happenings including *Lummox's* Canadian launches at http://okunhill.wordpress.com/

By Debbie Okun Hill: *Drawing from Experience* (Big Pond Rumours Press, 2017), *Chalk Dust Clouds* (Beret Days Press, 2017), *Tarnished Trophies* (Windsor, Ontario: Black Moss Press, 2014), *Another Trail of Comet Dust* (Beret Days Press, 2011), and *Swaddled in Comet Dust* (Beret Days Press, 2008).

Eryn Hiscock's writing has been published in literary journals and anthologies in both Canada and the U.S. She's a regular contributor of pop culture and lifestyle articles to online publications. She's presently at work on the same speculative fiction novel she's been trying to write for years.

Lawrence Hopperton lives in Stouffville, Ontario. Former editor of the *University of Toronto Review,* and founding editor of Nimbus Press, his poetry has been published internationally, most recently in the fifth *Lummox* anthology, *Sirsee, Sheila-Na-Gig, Smeuse,* and *Pocket Change.* He has published two chapbooks, *Songs of Orkney and Other Poems* in 1983, and *Ptolley Bay* in 2013. He has also written three college textbooks and many academic papers. He works as Director of Distributed Learning at Tyndale University College & Seminary.

By Lawrence Hopperton: *Ptolley Bay* (Toronto: Lyricalmyrical, 2013) and *Songs of Orkney and Other Poems* (1983).

Laurence Hutchman grew up in Toronto, receiving his BA from Western University in London, Ontario, an MA from Concordia in Montreal and a PhD from the Université de Montreal. He has taught at a number of universities including Concordia University, The University of Alberta, Western University, and the Université de Moncton at the Edmundston Campus were he was a professor for 23 years. He also served as President of the Writers' Federation of New Brunswick and co-organized the Alden Nowlan Literary Festival. Hutchman has published ten books of poetry, co-edited the anthology *Coastlines: the Poetry of Atlantic Canada*, and edited *In the Writers' Words*. His poetry has received numerous grants and awards, including the Alden Nowlan Award for Excellence, and his poems have been translated into French, Spanish, Dutch, Italian, Polish, Bangla, and Chinese. His most recent book is *Two Maps of Emery*. Last year he was named poet laureate of Emery, north Toronto. He lives with his wife, the artist and poet, Eva Kolacz in Oakville.

By Laurence Hutchman: POETRY: *Two Maps of Emery* (Windsor: Black Moss Press, 2016), *Personal Encounters* (Windsor: Black Moss Press, 2014), *Reading the Water* (Windsor: Black Moss Press, 2008), *Selected Poems* (Toronto: Guernica Editions, 2007), *Beyond Borders*: (Fredericton, New Brunswick: Broken Jaw Press, 2000), *Emery* (Windsor: Black Moss Press, 1998), *Foreign National* (Ottawa: Agawa Press, 1993), *Blue Riders* (Montreal: Maker Press, 1985), *Explorations* (Montreal: D.C. Books, 1975), and *The Twilight Kingdom* (London: Killaly Press, 1973); PROSE: *In the Writers' Words: Conversations with Eight Canadian Poets* (Toronto: Guernica Editions, 2011).

Luciano Iacobelli is a Toronto poet, visual artist, editor, and publisher. He is very active in the Toronto poetry scene as both an event organizer and publisher. He was a founder of the Wordstage reading series (2005-2013) along with Allan Briesmaster, Beatriz Hausner, and John Calabro. With the same partners, he founded Quattro Books and is now the sole owner and executive director of the press. Through Lyricalmyrical Press, his personal micropress specializing in handmade chapbooks, he has published many new voices along with established ones. Iacobelli is the author of 4 full length books of poetry, and co-authored a text of experimental poetry entitled *The Emu Dialogues* with Jens Kohler and Robert Marra. His work has been translated into Italian, Spanish, and French. His poems and essays have appeared in various journals and magazines.

By Luciano Iacobelli: *The Examined Life* (Toronto: Guernica Editions, 2016), *The Emu Dialogues*, with Jens Kohler and Robert Marra (Toronto: Quattro Books, 2015), *Painting Circles* (Mexico: Mantis Editores, 2012), *Book of Disorders* (Toronto: Quattro Books, 2011), and *The Angel Notebook* (Seraphim Editions, 2007).

Keith Inman was a steamfitter in a paper mill, where he fit steam into small spaces, then, had it *leap back out* as water, like a circus animal. He has no formal training in literature, save some night classes at Brock University and Niagara College, and a one-week course on Joyce at UCD Dublin. His faith in writing comes from individual teachers, especially *one* who took him to museums to look at the way French and Canadian impressionism worked. Inman's art tends to set binary forces of place, character, and circumstance in each other's way allowing the drama/action to happen. This poetic style was compared to fictional works by Atwood, Boyden, and Itani (Canlit 223). He has won a handful of awards, and grants from his peers. Copies of his work have been shared across Canada, the U.S., Cuba, and Ireland. One collection, *The War Poems: Screaming at Heaven*, can be found in major University libraries across North America. Home is the inland port of Thorold, Ontario, where huge ships climb the continent.

By Keith Inman: *SEAsia* (Windsor, Ontario: Black Moss Press, 2017), *The War Poems: Screaming at Heaven* (Windsor, Ontario: Black Moss Press, 2014), *Layers of Limestone* (Niagara Falls, Ontario: Grey Borders Books, 2015), *Hanging on a Nail* (Fort Erie, Ontario: Sigilate Press, 2009), and *Tactile Hunters* (Niagara Falls, Ontario: Cubicle Press, 2005).

Susan Ioannou has lived in Toronto since her birth in 1944; her fiction, articles, and poetry have appeared across Canada. She is the winner of an Okanagan Short Story Award, twice a finalist in the Canadian Broadcasting Corporation Literary Awards, and the recipient of a Works in Progress and Writers' Reserve grants from the Ontario Arts Council. Some of her poems have been translated into Hindi and Dutch, and others set to music for performance in both Canada and Norway. Her more recent poetry collections include *Looking Through Stone: Poems about the Earth* on geology, metals, minerals, and mining history, and *Looking for Light* in search of beauty and meaning in a troubled world. For many years she was Associate Editor of *Cross-Canada Writers' Quarterly/Magazine* and also led writing workshops for the Toronto Board of Education, the Ryerson University Literary Society, and the University of Toronto School of Continuing Studies. She is a longstanding member of The League of Canadian Poets and The Writers' Union of Canada. Her website is http://www.susanioannou.ca

By Susan Ioannou: POETRY: *Looking for Light* (Brighton, Ontario: Hidden Brook Press, 2016), *Looking Through Stone: Poems about the Earth* (Sudbury, Ontario: Your Scrivener Press, 2007), *The Merla Poems* (Toronto: Wordwrights Canada, 2006), *Who Would Be a God? A Debate in Poetry*, with Lenny Everson (Kitchener, Ontario: Passion Among the Cacti Press, 2004), *Coming Home: An Old Love Story* (Lantzville, British Columbia: Leaf Press, 2004), *Where the Light Waits* (Victoria, British Columbia: Ekstasis Editions, 1996), *Clarity Between Clouds* (Fredericton, New Brunswick: Goose Lane Editions, 1991), *Familiar Faces/Private Grief* (Toronto: Wordwrights Canada, 1986), *Motherpoems* (Toronto: Wordwrights Canada: 1985), and *Spare Words* (Brandon, Manitoba: Pierian Press, 1984); PROSE: *Writing Reader-friendly Poems Plus Writing Exercises* (Toronto: Wordwrights Canada, 2011), *The Hidden Valley Mystery* (Toronto: Wordwrights Canada, 2010), *Nine to Ninety: Stories across the generations* (Toronto: Wordwrights Canada, 2009),

Holding True: Essays on Being a Writer (Toronto: Wordwrights Canada, 2008), *Read-Aloud Poems: For Students from Elementary Through Senior High School* (Toronto: Wordwrights Canada, 2001), *A Magical Clockwork: The Art of Writing the Poem* (Toronto: Wordwrights Canada, 2000), *Polly's Punctuation Primer* (Toronto: Wordwrights Canada, 1994), and *The Crafted Poem: A Step by Step Guide to Writing and Appreciation* (Toronto: Wordwrights Canada, 1994).

I.B. (Bunny) Iskov is the Founder of The Ontario Poetry Society, www.theontariopoetrysociety.ca. Bunny has won a few contest prizes and she has several poetry collections. She is the recipient of the Absolutely Fabulous Woman Award, Arts & Culture category, 2017.

Ellen S. Jaffe grew up in New York City, lived in London, U.K. for several years, then immigrated to Canada in 1979. She has lived in Hamilton, Ontario since 2000. Her poetry collection, *Skinny-Dipping with the Muse* (Guernica Editions, 2014) was nominated for the 2015 Hamilton Literary Awards. Other books include *Water Children* (poetry), which won a Hamilton Literary Award in 2003, *Feast of Lights* (young adult novel), and *Writing Your Way,* on writing practice. Her poetry has appeared in anthologies including *Crossing Lines: Poets Who Came to Canada in the Vietnam War Era* and *Jack Layton: Art and Action*, and many Canadian journals. She has given readings in Hamilton, Toronto, Prince Edward Island, and British Columbia, and a bilingual chapbook of her poems was published in Helsinki, Finland in 2005, by the Therapeia Foundation. With her colleague Lil Blume, Ellen co-organized 3 Canadian Jewish Literary Festivals in Hamilton and published accompanying anthologies. She teaches writing in schools and community centres, and was nominated for a City of Hamilton Arts Award in writing, 2017.

By Ellen S. Jaffe: POETRY: *Skinny-Dipping With the Muse* (Toronto: Guernica Editions, 2014), *Twelve Moons and Six More Poems* (2010), *Syntymalauluja/Birthsongs*, poems translated into Finnish (2005), and *Water Children* (2002); FICTION: *Feast of Lights* (2006); DRAMA: *Promise You Won't Marry Me* (2008) and *Jason's Quest* (2001); NON-FICTION: *Writing Your Way: Creating a Personal Journal* (2001).

Carol Keller is a lifelong resident in the province of Saskatchewan. She was raised in a small town 40 minutes away from her current residence in North Battleford, and has lived the last twenty-five years in the Battlefords with her husband and five children. She is a writer who has attempted poetry, essay, short story, creative non-fiction novella and recently a manuscript for a young adult fiction novel.

Eva Kolacz is a poet and painter whose works are inspired by the multifaceted nature of both the interior and exterior world. She debuted as a young poet in local magazines and became a member of a writers' association in her native Poland. After she immigrated to Canada in 1981, she continued to write and publish poems in Polish like *Variety: Rozmaitosci, Gazetta, High Park* and in an anthology with the Polish-American Academy based in New Jersey. In English she has published in *Verse-Afire, Rapsodia*, and she was the feature artist in the inaugural issue of *The Artis*. After graduating from the Fine Arts Department of the Ontario College of Art and Design in Toronto, she participated in numerous exhibitions in Canada, the United States, and Europe. Her works have become part of the permanent collections of the Ontario government and major museums of Poland. She lives and works in Oakville with her husband, the poet Laurence Hutchman. She is a member of The Ontario Poetry Society and the Polish American Poets Academy.

Maureen Korp is a military brat, the daughter of an American soldier. She grew up in faraway places; including, Okinawa, Hokkaido, Oklahoma, Texas, and Germany. Home base today is Ottawa. She travels with a Canadian passport, happily. Maureen Korp is an independent scholar, critic, curator, and lecturer. She has taught at universities in the United States, Canada, Romania, and, most recently, Pakistan (2008-'10). Her field of research is visionary earth-centered beliefs and art. She has curated highly regarded exhibitions of contemporary art in Canada, the United States, Romania, and Pakistan. Maureen Korp is the author of three books, 16 exhibition catalogues, more than 125 articles. Her poems have appeared in a number of Canadian poetry journals, including, *Antigonish Review, Arc, Canadian Forum, Cross-Canada Writers' Quarterly, Matrix, Quarry, Queen's Quarterly,* and *Vallum*.

By Maureen Korp: *Sacred Art of the Earth: Ancient and Contemporary Earthworks* (Continuum, 1997) and *The Sacred Geography of the American Mound Builders* (Edwin Mellen Press, 1990).

Laurie Kruk teaches at Nipissing University, where she is Full Professor in English Studies. She specializes in Canadian Literature, Native Literature, Women's writing, and the Canadian short story. As a scholar, Kruk has published *The Voice is the Story: Conversations with Canadian Writers of Short Fiction* and *Double-Voicing the Canadian Short Story*. She is also the author of three books of poetry: *Theories of the World, Loving the Alien,* and *My Mother Did Not Tell Stories*. Most recently, Kruk has co-edited *Borderlands and Crossroads: Writing the Motherland* (Demeter, 2016), a creative anthology, with poet Jane Satterfield. The idea of 'Borderlands and Crossroads' appeared a natural fit for our shared interest, as women co-editors, in how our lives change, grow, and enlarge, through the act of mothering, whether adoptive mothers, biological mothers, stepmothers, or 'other-mothers'." Kruk also finds inspiration in her Northern Ontario "Camp" at River Valley. A member of the Near North Voices Choir, she was featured as a poet, with a reading of her poem, "The Temagami Speaks: June" at the "Northern Lights" concert held in North Bay.

By Laurie Kruk: POETRY: *My Mother Did Not Tell Stories* (Demeter, 2012), *Loving the Alien* (YSP, 2006), and *Theories of the World* (Netherlandic, 1992); PROSE: *Double-Voicing the Canadian Short Story* (Ottawa UP, 2016) and *The Voice is the Story: Conversations with Canadian Writers of Short Fiction* (Oakville, Ontario: Mosaic Press, 2003).

Donna Langevin's latest poetry collections include *In the Café du Monde*, Hidden Brook Press 2008, and *The Laundress of Time,* Aeolus House 2014. Her next book of poetry is forthcoming from Piquant Press in 2018. Her poems have been published in numerous journals such as *Arc*, *The Antigonish Review*, *CV2*, *Descant*, and *Grain*. Her awards include: first prize in a TOPS Contest 2008 and also in the Cyclamens and Swords contest 2009. Short-listed for the *Descant* 2010 Winston Collins prize in 2012, she won second prize in the Hamilton GritLIT contest 2014, and in the Banister Anthology Competition 2017. Donna's play productions include, *The Man with a Butterfly Hat* (Toronto Alumnae Theatre, 2012 NIF Festival) and *Welcome to Nuit Blanche* (Ryerson 50+ Festival, 2014). *The Dinner*, published by *Morel* magazine, won first prize in the play script contest at the Eden Mills Writers' Festival 2014, as did *Bargains in the New World* in 2015. *If Socrates Were in My Shoes* was produced in the NIF festival, 2018.

By Donna Langevin: *The Laundress of Time* (Aeolus House, 2015), *Looking for Yesterday* (Lyricalmyrical, 2013), *The Middle-aged Man in the Sea* (Lyricalmyrical, 2009), *In the Café du Monde* (Hidden Brook Press, 2008), *The Second Language of Birds* (Hidden Brook Press, 2005), *Songbirds of the Hours* (Fooliar Press, 2004), and *Improvising in the Dark* (watershedBooks, 2000).

Ruth Latta has won first and second prizes in the annual contest held by the Canadian Authors' Association, National Capital Branch. Her poetry has appeared in various North American publications, including several published by The Ontario Poetry Society. She included eight of her own poems in her young adult novel, *The Songcatcher and Me* (Ottawa: Baico, 2013). She has published eighteen books, which include history, biography, short story collections, and novels. Her 2011 short story collection, *Winter Moon*, won the "Northern Lit" award for English fiction from Ontario Library Services North. Ruth lives in Ottawa, Ontario with her husband, Roger Latta, and her cat, Lily. For more information, visit http://ruthlattabooks.blogspot.ca and http://ruthlatta.blogspot.ca

By Ruth Latta: POETRY: *Polarities*, with Valerie Simmons, *How We Flushed Fluffy*, with Valerie Simmons, *Encore*, with Valerie Simmons, and *How to Remember*; FICTION: *Grace in Love* (Ottawa: Baico, 2018), *Grace and the Secret Vault* (Ottawa: Baico, 2017), *Most of All* (Amazon Kindle, 2015), *The Songcatcher and Me* (Ottawa: Baico, 2013), *The Old Love and the New Love* (Ottawa: Baico, 2011), *Winter Moon* (Ottawa: Baico, 2010), *Spelling Bee* (Ottawa: Baico, 2009), *An Amethyst Remembrance* (Ottawa: Baico, 2008), *Memories Stick* (Ottawa: Baico, 2007),

Illusions Die (Ottawa: Baico, 2006), *The Secret of White Birch Road* (Ottawa: Baico, 2005), *Tea With Delilah* (2004), *Save The Last Dance for Me* (Poetica Press, 2002), *Life Music* (1998), and *A Wild Streak* (General Store, 1995); NON-FICTION: *They Tried: the Story of the Canadian Youth Congress* (2006), *Grace MacInnis: A Woman to Remember* (Xlibris, 2001), *The Memory of All That* (General Store, 1993), and *Life Writing* (General Store, 1988).

Beth Learn is a multi-media and interdisciplinary language artist currently living in Toronto. She is the former Associate Editor of *Queen Street Magazine*, a past Director of the Kensington Arts Association (KAA Gallery), and was Production Coordinator for "The Language and Structure in North America" exhibition at the 567 Gallery in Toronto in 1975. Since 1974 she has worked under the name learn/yeats & co to produce much of her work as an artist including the publication of her books of poetic text (*alice springs, sabbath moon, Entrance of Albert Ruz,* and *Sister Squares etc*), as well as publication/production of *Cabaret Vert Magazine* and associate languages shows. learn/yeats & co continues the ongoing art/science investigation known as the *alice springs project,* which involves the "Contextural" analysis of language fields or texts as found in her collection of 15 poems, *alice springs*. She continues to read and work with her daughter, Joy Learn, who is also an artist and Associate Editor of *Cabaret Vert Magazine*. Email: blearn@learnyeats.com. Website: http://learnyeats.com/index.htm.

By Beth Learn: *on loan from collection of the artist, alice springs, sabbath moon, The Wooden Thistle, wild dog woods, In the Laboratory of the Psychologist, The List of Missing Authorities, Rene: Therefore I am where the trouble is, Bell: How much a matter of fact the given is, Parenthesis, Between Positions of Opposition, the Concept of Sister Squares, The Entrance of Albert Ruz,* and *Bethie at the Beach*. (All books published in Toronto by learn/yeats & co.)

John B. Lee was inducted as Poet Laureate of Brantford in perpetuity in 2005. In 2007 he was made a member of the Chancellor's Circle of the President's Club of McMaster University, and was named winner of the inaugural Black Moss Press *Souwesto Award* for his contribution to the ethos of writing in Southwestern Ontario. In 2011 he was appointed Poet Laureate of Norfolk County (2011-14), and in 2015 Honourary Poet Laureate of Norfolk County for life, and in 2017 he received a Canada 150 Medal from the Federal Government of Canada for "his outstanding contribution to literary development both at home and abroad." A winner of the $10,000 CBC Literary Award for Poetry, Lee is the only two time recipient of the Milton Acorn Memorial People's Poetry Award. He has well-over seventy books published. His work has appeared internationally in over 500 publications and has been translated into French, Spanish, Korean, and Chinese. Called "the greatest living poet in English," by poet George Whipple, Lee lives in Port Dover, Ontario where he works as a full time author.

By John B. Lee: POETRY: *These are the Words: Bread Water Love* (Hidden Brook Press, 2018), *Into a Land of Strangers* (Mosaic Press, 2018), *Beautiful Stupid: selected and new 2001-2017* (Black Moss Press, 2018), *The Sesquicentennial Poems: Tai Grove and John B. Lee* (Sanbun Publishing, 2018), *This is How We See the World: the chapbook years* (Hidden Brook Press, 2017), *Secret Second Language of the Heart* (Sanbun Publishing, 2016), *The Full Measure* (Black Moss Press, 2015), *Adoration of the Unnecessary* (Beret Days Press, 2015), *Burning My Father* (Black Moss Press, 2014), *In This We Hear the Light* (Hidden Brook Press, 2013), *Let Us Be Silent Here* (Sanbun Publishing, 2012), *In the Muddy Shoes of Morning* (Hidden Brook Press, 2010), *Dressed in Dead Uncles* (Black Moss Press, 2010), *Being Human* (Sunbun Press, 2012), *One Leaf in the Breath of the World* (Beret Days Press, 2009), *Let Light Try All the Doors* (Rubicon Press, 2009), *Island on the Wind-Breathed Edge of the Sea* (Hidden Brook Press, 2008), *The Place that We Keep After Leaving* (Black Moss Press, 2008), *But Where Were the Horses of Evening* (Serengeti Press, 2007), *Godspeed* (Black Moss Press, 2006), *How Beautiful We Are* (Black Moss Press, 2006), *Poems for the Pornographer's Daughter* (Black Moss Press, 2005), *Bright Red Apples of the Dead* (Pooka Press, 2004), *Though Their Joined Hearts Drummed Like Larks* (Passion Among the Cacti Press, 2004), *Thirty-Three Thousand Shades of Green* (Leaf Press, 2004), *Totally Unused Heart* (Black Moss Press, 2003), *The Hockey Player Sonnets: overtime edition* (Penumbra Press, 2003), *In the Terrible Weather of Guns* (Mansfield Press, 2002), *The Half-Way Tree: selected poems* (Black Moss Press, 2001), *An Almost Silent Drumming: the South Africa poems* (Cranberry Tree Press, 2001), *Don't Be So Persnickety* (Black Moss Press, 2000), *Stella's Journey* (Black Moss Press, 1999), *Soldier's Heart* (Black Moss Press, 1998), *The Echo of Your Words Has Reached Me*, (Mekler & Deahl Publishers, 1998), *Never Hand Me Anything if I am Walking or Standing*, (Black Moss Press, 1997), *In a Language with No Word For Horses* (above/ground press, 1997), *Tongues of the Children* (Black Moss Press, 1996), *The Day Jane Fonda Came to Guelph* (The Ploughman Press, 1996), *The Beatles Landed Laughing in New York* (Black Moss Press, 1995), *These Are the Days of Dogs and Horses* (Black Moss Press, 1994), *All the Cats Are Gone* (Penumbra Press, 1993), *Variations on Herb* (Brick Books, 1993), *The Art of Walking Backwards* (Black Moss Press, 1993), *When Shaving Seems Like Suicide* (Goose Lane Editions, 1992), *The Pig Dance Dreams* (Black Moss Press, 1991), *The Hockey Player Sonnets* (Penumbra Press, 1991), *The Bad Philosophy of Good Cows* (Black Moss Press, 1989), *Rediscovered Sheep* (Brick Books, 1987), *Hired Hands* (Brick Books, 1986), *Small Worlds* (Vesta Publications, 1986), *Fossils of the Twentieth Century* (Vesta Publications, 1983), *To Kill a White Dog* (Brick Books, 1982), *Love Among the Tombstones* (Dogwood Press, 1980), and *Poems Only A Dog Could Love* (Applegarth Follies, 1976); PROSE: *The Widow's Land: superstition and farming—a madness of daughters* (Black Moss Press, 2016), *You Can Always Eat the Dogs: the hockeyness of ordinary men* (Black Moss Press, 2012), *King Joe: A Matter of Treason—the life and times of Joseph Willcocks (1773-September 5, 1814)* (Heronwood Enterprises, 2011), *Left Hand Horses: meditations on influence and the imagination*, (Black Moss Press, 2007), *The Farm on the Hill He Calls Home* (Black Moss Press, 2004), *Building Bicycles in the Dark: a practical guide to writing* (Black Moss Press,

2001), *What's in a Name: the pursuit of George Peacock, Namesake of Peacock Point* (Dogwood Press, 1996), *Head Heart Hands Health: A History of 4H in Ontario* (Comrie Productions, 1994); TRANSLATION: *Sweet Cuba: Three-Hundred Years of Cuban poetry in Spanish and in English translation* — John B. Lee and Manuel de Jesus (Hidden Brook Press, 2010).

Bernice Lever has read her poems on 5 continents and her 10th poetry book is *Small Acts* (Black Moss Press, 2016). A retired college English teacher and freelance editor, she lives on Bowen Island, British Columbia. Bernice edited *WAVES, Fine Canadian Writing* (1972 - 1987) at York University. She is a Life Member of the Canadian Writers Association and of the League of Canadian Poets, as well as long time member of Federation of BC Writers and other groups. Also she has won many awards and prizes, but is proudest to be an international Peace Poet. Her WebSite is: www.colourofwords.com

By Bernice Lever: *Small Acts* (Black Moss Press, 2016), *Red Letter Day* (Black Moss Press, 2014), *Imagining Lives* (Black Moss Press, 2012), *Generation* (Black Moss Press, 2009), *Never a Straight Line* (Black Moss Press, 2007), *Blessings* (Black Moss Press, 2000), *Things Unsaid* (Black Moss Press, 1996), *The Waiting Room* (Highway Book Shop, 1993), *Sometimes the Distance* (Mosaic Press, 1986), *Yet, Woman I Am* (Highway Book Shop, 1979), and *Excuses For All Occasions* (Highway Book Shop, 1979).

Norma West Linder was born in Toronto, spent her childhood on Manitoulin Island, and her teenage years in Muskoka. She is a member of The Writers' Union of Canada, PEN, The Ontario Poetry Society, WIT (Writers in Transition), After Hours Poets, and is a Past President of the Sarnia Branch of the Canadian Authors Association. Linder is the author of 6 novels, 15 collections of poetry, a memoir of Manitoulin Island, two children's books, and a biography of Pauline McGibbon. For 24 years she was on the faculty of Lambton College, teaching English and Creative Writing. For 7 years she wrote a monthly column for the *Sarnia Observer*. Her short stories have been published internationally and broadcast on the CBC. Her poetry has been published in *The Fiddlehead, White Wall Review, Room of One's Own, Quills, Toward the Light, The Prairie Journal, FreeFall Magazine, Mobius*, and other periodicals. Her latest poetry publications are *Two Paths Through The Seasons* (with James Deahl) and a selected poems, *Adder's-tongues*. She has two daughters and a son.

By Norma West Linder: POETRY: *Two Paths Through The Seasons*, with James Deahl (Metulla, Israel: Cyclamens and Swords, 2014), *Adder's-tongues* (Thornhill, Ontario: Aeolus House, 2012), *Lovely as a Tree* (Thornhill, Ontario: Beret Days Press, 2010), *When Angels Weep* (Thornhill, Ontario: Beret Days Press, 2009), *Days of Draper Township School SS#1* (Thornhill, Ontario: Beret Days Press, 2007), *Magical Manitoulin* (Thornhill, Ontario: Beret Days Press, 2006),

River of Lethe (East Hawkesbury, Ontario: Poets' Podium, 2003), *Jazz in The Old Orange Hall* (Sarnia, Ontario: River City Press, 1999), *Morning Child* (Sarnia, Ontario: River City Press, 1995), *Matter of Life and Death* (Brandon, Manitoba: Brandon University's Pierian Press, 1985), *The Rooming House* (Sarnia, Ontario: River City Press, 1983), *This Age of Reason* (London, Ontario: South Western Ontario Poetry, 1982), *Pyramid* (Sarnia, Ontario: Lambton College, 1980), *Ring Around The Sun* (Cornwall, Ontario: Vesta Publications, 1976), and *On The Side of The Angels* (Fredericton, New Brunswick: Fiddlehead Poetry Books, 1971); FICTION: *Tall Stuff* (Brighton, Ontario: Hidden Brook Press, 2016), *No Common Thread: The Selected Short Fiction* (Brighton, Ontario: Hidden Brook Press, 2013), *The Savage Blood* (Sarnia, Ontario: River City Press, 1987), *Woman in a Blue Hat* (Markham, Ontario: Simon & Schuster, 1977), *Nahanni* (with Hope Morritt) (London, England: Robert Hale & Co., 1975), *Tangled Butterflies* (London, England: Robert Hale & Co., 1974), and *The Lemon Tree* (Toronto: Nelson, Foster & Scott, 1973); CHILDREN'S BOOKS: *The Pastel Planet* (Brighton, Ontario: Hidden Brook Press, 2015) and *Corey* (Cornwall, Ontario: Vesta Publications, 1979): BIOGRAPHY: *Pauline: A Warm Look at Ontario Lt. Gov. Pauline McGibbon* (with Hope Morritt) (Sarnia, Ontario: River City Press, 1979); MEMOIR: *Morels and Maple Syrup* (Cornwall, Ontario: Vesta Publications, 1977).

Annick MacAskill is a Canadian poet and reviewer whose writing has appeared in Canadian and international journals, including *Prism international, Versal, Room Magazine*, *PANK*, *The Fiddlehead, Arc Poetry Magazine*, and *Bone Bouquet*. She is the author of a chapbook, *Brotherly Love: Poems of Sappho and Charaxos* (Frog Hollow Press, 2016), as well as a forthcoming full-length debut (Gaspereau Press, 2018).

By Annick MacAskill: *Brotherly Love: Poems of Sappho and Charaxos* (Frog Hollow Press, 2016).

Carol Malyon is a Toronto writer of poetry, short stories, and novels. She is an ex-bookseller, and prefers minimalism in both her reading material and her own writing. She has been writer-in-residence at the University of New Brunswick, and led short story workshops in North Bay, Ontario and Fredericton, New Brunswick.

By Carol Malyon: POETRY: *Colville's People, Headstand*, and *Emma's Dead*; FICTION: *The Adultery Handbook, The Migration of Butterflies, Cathedral Women, If I Knew I'd Tell You, The Edge of the World*, and *Lovers & Other Strangers*: OTHER: *Mixed-up Grandmas* (for children) and *Griddle Talk*, with bill bisssett (non-fiction).

Blaine Marchand's award winning poetry and prose has appeared in magazines across Canada, the U.S., and Pakistan. He has been active in the literary scene in his home city,

Ottawa, for over 40 years and has six books of poetry published, a chapbook, a children's novel, and a work of non-fiction; was President of the League of Canadian Poets from 1991-93; and, was a monthly columnist for Capital XTRA, the LGTBQ2 community paper, for nine years. His writing has been influenced by his work and travels in Africa and Asia. Following a two-year diplomatic posting in Islamabad, Pakistan, he co-edited with Pakistani poet and artist, Ilona Yusuf, a special *Vallum* poetry magazine issue devoted to Pakistani poets writing in English (*Vallum* 9:1 "Poets from Pakistan", 2012). In April 2017, he participated in the Islamabad Literary Festival and his work has been profiled in two prestigious Pakistani literary journals. He is at work on a new manuscript of poems, *Where You Dwell*, and on a collection of short stories, *Nomads*.

By Blaine Marchand: POETRY: *My Head, Filled with Pakistan* (catkin press, 2016), *The Craving of Knives* (BuschekBooks, 2009), *Aperture* (BuschekBooks, 2008), *Bodily Presence* (Quarry Press, 1995), *A Garden Enclosed* (Cormorant Press, 1991), *Open Fires* (Anthos Press, 1987), and *After the Fact* (Borealis Press, 1980); PROSE: *African Journey* (Mediasphere, 1990) and *Ottawa, A to Z* (Duneau Press, 1979).

Steven McCabe is the author of four full-length poetry collections. His work is included in a number of anthologies. His most recent book is a 'wordless poem' *Never More Together* published by The Porcupine's Quill and comprised of 120 linocut prints 'showing' a speculative poem about the surveillance state intersecting with prehistory & the Garden of Eden. Across the years he has mounted solo gallery exhibitions featuring ink drawings, paintings on canvas, assemblage, and video. He is the creator of the Wordpress blog *poemimage,* addressing international and Canadian poetry, as well as his own, with digital art. He has created six poetry films in creative collaboration with time-based media technicians. Currently he is at work on a surrealistic novel as well as a collection of non-fiction stories featuring synchronicity, high strangeness, and humour. After a long break from the book-form of poetic text to focus on video, he is now assembling a manuscript influenced by the Neolithic & ancient Europe. Steven McCabe lives in Toronto, Ontario.

By Steven McCabe: *Never More Together* (The Porcupine's Quill, 2014), *Hierarchy of Loss* (Ekstasis Editions, 2007), *Orpheus and Eurydice: Before the Descent*, with T. Nanavati (Lyricalmyrical, 2006), *Jawbone* (Ekstasis Editions, 2005), *Radio Picasso* (watershedBooks, 1999) and *Wyatt Earp in Dallas: 1963* (Seraphim Editions, 1996).

Elizabeth McCallister grew up in Scarborough and moved to Saskatoon where she worked with several of the Writers-in-Residence at the Saskatoon Public Library. Back in 2001, she attended the Sage Hill Writing Experience. She moved back to Ontario in 2002 and now resides in

Brantford. Her *Notes from Suburbia* was published by Craigleigh Press in 2013. She is currently a member of the Ontario Poetry Society and the Brantford Poetry Society.

By Elizabeth McCallister: *Notes from Suburbia* (Cambridge, Ontario: Craigleigh Press, 2013).

Mori McCrae is a Fine Arts graduate of the Ontario College of Art, specializing in drawing and painting. She has lived and worked in the Niagara Region for the past twenty-seven years, developing strong ties to the region and the artistic community. Writing poetry followed her painting career, the "surprise" that arrived unexpectedly, late in life. *Shelf Life*, her debut chapbook was published in 2017. She is currently working on a new collection of poems called *Passersby*. Her interest focuses on the day to day experience of being human, through individualized, written portraits — a layering of vignettes that welcomes the universal, should it emerge. She lives with her husband and two dogs in a house accurately named "The Hobbit," in downtown St. Catharines, Ontario.

By Mori McCrae: *Shelf Life* and *Passersby* (both from: Grey Borders Books, Niagara Falls, Ontario).

Ian McCulloch lives in North Bay, Ontario where he has spent much of the last two decades enjoying his time as a stay-at-home Dad. He is a member of the Fox Lake Chapleau Cree and the author of several poetry collections and a novel, *Childforever*.

By Ian McCulloch: POETRY: *Balsam To Ease All Pains* (Alburnum Press, 1998), *Parables and Rain* (Penumbra Press, 1993), *The Efficiency of Killers* (Penumbra Press, 1988), and *The Moon of Hunger* (Penumbra Press, 1982); NOVEL: *Childforever* (Mercury Press, 1996).

Susan McMaster lives in Ottawa. She's a Past President of the League of Canadian Poets, has published some thirty books, anthologies, and wordmusic recordings with First Draft and Geode Music & Poetry. She founded Canada's first feminist magazine, *Branching Out*, and organized such projects as "Convergence: Poems for Peace", which brought poetry and art from across Canada to Parliament for the millennium. Her poetry has placed for the Ottawa Book Awards, Acorn-Plantos People's Poetry Prize, Archibald Lampman Award, and Montreal International Poetry Prize. Memberships include PEN Canada and The Writers' Union of Canada. Recent reviews: Carolyn Smart, McGill-Queen's: "McMaster's purview is the world entire, with all its mystery, heartbreak and magic." Heather Spears, Governor General's award winner: "Winsome, muscular, candid, intimate yet universal ... an open, seemingly effortless control of her craft ... startling, inevitable (and beautiful)." Dave Margoshes, director, Sage Hill writing program:

"Deceptively simple poems, but there's nothing deceptive about their craftsmanship or their honesty. The best ones ease up to you, then sting." Jan Conn, poet: "There is rhythm and verve in every dimension McMaster explores."

By Susan McMaster: POETRY: *Haunt, Paper Affair: Poems Selected & New, Crossing Arcs: Alzheimer's, my mother, and me, Until the Light Bends, Ygdrasil: Selected Poems, La Deriva del Pianeta / World Shift* (Schifanoia, Italy), *Uncommon Prayer: A book of dedications, Learning to Ride, The Hummingbird Murders*, and *Dark Galaxies*; CREATIVE NON-FICTION: *The Gargoyle's Left Ear: Writing in Ottawa.*

Bronwen McRae was born and raised in Moose Jaw, Saskatchewan. She lives on an acreage near Pike Lake, Saskatchewan. Her work has appeared in the *Ottawa Arts Review, Room, spring, Transition, Blink Ink, The Prairie Journal*, and *The Society* as well as online at Leaf Press, *Your Daily Poem*, and *Blue Skies Poetry*. She has participated in the Saskatchewan Writer's Guild Mentorship Program and The Sage Hill Writing Experience. Bronwen is a founding member of the Obsessors Poetry Group, and recently completed her first poetry manuscript. When she is not writing, Bronwen works as a Preschool Teacher and enjoys cheering on The Saskatchewan Roughriders.

Rhonda Melanson is a graduate of Queen's University Artist In The Community Education Program. Rhonda has been published in several print and online magazines, including *The Boxcar Poetry Review, Quill's, Philadelphia Poets, Ascent Aspirations, Lummox* and the *Windsor Review*. In 2011, she published a chapbook called *Gracenotes* with Beret Days Press, and she is also featured in the *Encompass IV* anthology, a publication from Beret Days Press and The Ontario Poetry Society. Recently, she was featured in *Nasty Women and Bad Hombres*, A Poetry Anthology, edited by Deena November and Nina Padolf (Lascaux Editions).

By Rhonda Melanson: *Gracenotes* (Beret Days Press).

Bruce Meyer is author or editor of 63 books including the national bestsellers *The Golden Thread* (2000), and *Portraits of Canadian Writers* (2016). His most recent books are *1967: Centennial Year* (poetry) and *A Feast of Brief Hopes* (short fiction). He was the inaugural Poet Laureate of the City of Barrie and teaches at Georgian College in Barrie and at Victoria College in Toronto.

By Bruce Meyer: POETRY: *1967: Centennial Year* (Black Moss Press, 2017), *To Linares* (Accento and Universidad Technologica Linares, 2016), *The Madness of Planets* (Black Moss

Press, 2015), *The Arrow of Time* (Ronsdale Press, 2015), *The Seasons* (The Porcupine's Quill, 2014), *Testing the Elements* (Exile Editions, 2014), *The Obession Book of Timbuktu* (Black Moss Press), *A Litany of the Makers* (Lyricalmyrical, 2014), *A Book of Bread* (Exile Editions, 2011), *Alphabestiary: A Poetry Emblem Book* (Exile Editions, 2011), *Bread: A Mass for Voices* (Lyricalmyrical, 2009), *Dog Days: A Comedy of Terriers* (Black Moss Press, 2009), *Mesopotamia* (Scrivener Press, 2009), *As Yet, Untitled...* (Lyricalmyrical, 2006), *Oceans* (Word Press, 2005), *Oceans* (Exile Editions, 2004), *The Spirit Bride* (Exile Editions, 2002), *Anywhere* (Exile Editions, 2000), *The Presence* (Black Moss Press, 1999), *The Presence* (Story Line Press, 1999), *Radio Silence* (Black Moss Press, 1991), *The Open Room* (Black Moss Press, 1989), *The Open Room* (Aquilla Press, 1989), *Steel Valley* (Aureole Point Press, 1984), *The Aging of America* (Aloysius Press, 1982), and *The Tongues Between Us* (South Western Ontario Poetry, 1981); FICTION: *A Feast of Brief Hopes* (Guernica Editions, 2018), *A Chronicle of Magpies* (Tightrope Books, 2014), *Flights* (Canadian-Korean Literary Forum Press, 2004), and *Goodbye Mr. Spalding* (Black Moss Press, 1996); NON-FICTION: *The Shadow at Our Heels: Dogs and the Literary Imagination* (Biblioasis, 2018), *Portraits of Canadian Writers* (The Porcupine's Quill, 2016), *Time of the Last Goal: Why Hockey is Our Game* (Black Moss Press), *Alphabet Table: Memoir of a Childhood in the Language* (Black Moss Press, 2010), *Heroes: The Champions of Our Literary Imaginations* (HarperCollins, 2007), *The American New Formalists: Dictionary of Literary Biography* (Volume 282) (Bruccoli, Clarke, Layman, 2003), *The Golden Thread: A Reader's Journey Through the Great Books* (HarperCollins, 2000), *Lives and Works*: *Interviews with Canadian Writers* (Black Moss Press, 1991), and *In Their Words: Interviews with Canadian Writers* (Anansi, 1985).

Michael Mirolla describes his writing as a mix of magic realism, surrealism, speculative fiction, and meta-fiction. Publications include the novel *Berlin* (2010 Bressani Prize winner), *The Facility*, featuring a string of cloned Mussolinis, and *The Giulio Metaphysics III*, where "Giulio" battles for freedom from his own creator. Other publications: the short story collection *The Formal Logic of Emotion*; a punk novella, *The Ballad of Martin B.*; and two collections of poetry: *Light and Time* and *The House on 14th Avenue* (2014 Bressani Prize). His short story collection, *Lessons in Relationship Dyads* (Red Hen Press, California), took the 2016 Bressani Prize. The novel *Torp: The Landlord, The Husband, The Wife and The Lover*, set in 1970 Vancouver, was published in 2016, and 2017 saw the publication of the magic realist short story collection *The Photographer in Search of Death*. The short story, "A Theory of Discontinuous Existence," was selected for *The Journey Prize Anthology*, and "The Sand Flea" was a Pushcart Prize nominee. Born in Italy, raised in Montreal, Michael now lives in Oakville, Ontario. For more: http://www.michaelmirolla.com/index.html.

By Michael Mirolla: POETRY: *The House on 14th Avenue* (Signature Editions, 2013), *Light and Time* (Guernica Editions, 2010), *Interstellar Distances/Distanze Interstellari* (Il Grappolo, 2009), and

Chapbook Poems (Disposable Paper Press, 1974); FICTION: *The Photographer in Search of Death* (Exile Editions, 2017), *Torp* (Linda Leith Publishing, 2016), *Lessons in Relationship Dyads* (Red Hen Press, 2015), *The Giulio Metaphysics III* (Leapfrog Press, 2013), *The Ballad of Martin B* (Quattro Books, 2011), *The Facility* (Leapfrog Press, 2010), *La Logica formale delle emozioni* (Edarc Edizione, 2010), *Berlin* (Leapfrog Press, 2009), and *Hothouse Loves* (PublishAmerica, 2008).

Lynda Monahan is the author of three collections of poetry, *A Slow Dance in the Flames*, *What My Body Knows*, and *Verge*. She facilitates a number of creative writing workshops and has been writer-in-residence at St. Peter's College facilitated retreat, Balfour Collegiate in Regina and writer-in-residence at the Victoria Hospital in Prince Albert, Saskatchewan. She is editor of several collections including *Second Chances: stories of brain injury survivors*, *Skating in the Exit Light*, a poetry anthology, and *With Just One Reach of Hands*, an anthology of the writing of the Canadian Mental Health Association's Writing For Your Life group, which she also facilitates. She has served on the council for the League of Canadian Poets and on the boards of Sage Hill Writing Experience and the Saskatchewan Writers' Guild. She is currently writer-in-residence at the JM Cuelenaere Library in Prince Albert, Saskatchewan.

By Lynda Monahan: *A Slow Dance in the Flames* (Coteau Books), *What My Body Knows* (Coteau Books), and *Verge* (Guernica Editions).

A.F. Moritz's *The Sparrow: Selected Poems* appeared in spring 2018 from House of Anansi Press. Including it, he has written nineteen books of poetry, one of them, *Ciudad interior*, a selected poems in Spanish translation. He was chosen to the Princeton Series of Contemporary Poets (*The Tradition,* 1986); his poetry has received the Guggenheim Fellowship, the Ingram Merrill Fellowship, the Award in Literature of the American Academy of Arts and Letters, *Poetry* magazine's Beth Hokin Prize, etc. His poems have appeared in American magazines including *Poetry, Partisan Review, Paris Review, Hudson Review,* and *American Poetry Review,* and in four editions of *The Best American Poetry*. In Canada, his books have received the Griffin Poetry Prize, the ReLit Award, and the Raymond Souster Award, and have three times been finalists for the Governor General's Literary Award. His Griffin Poetry Prize-winning collection, *The Sentinel* (2008), was a *Toronto Globe and Mail* Top 100 Book of the Year, and his ReLit Award-winning *Night Street Repairs* (2004) was named one of forty-three "books of the decade" by the *Globe and Mail* in 2010.

By A.F. Moritz: BOOKS: *The Sparrow: Selected Poems* (Toronto: House of Anansi, 2018), *Sequence* (2015), *The New Measures* (2012), *The Sentinel* (2008), *Night Street Repairs* (2004), *Early Poems* (2002), *Conflicting Desire* (2001), *The End of the Age* (2000), *Rest on the Flight into Egypt* (1999), *Houseboat on the Styx* (1998), *Mahoning* (1994), *Phantoms in the Ark* (1994),

Ciudad interior (1993), *The Ruined Cottage* (1993), *Song of Fear* (1992), *The Tradition* (1986), *The Visitation* (1983), *Between the Root and the Flower* (1982), *Black Orchid* (1981), and *Here* (1974); 12 CHAPBOOKS: *The Sentinel, Crossroads Near Somewhere, Sound of Hungry Animals, Twelve Poems, Back to Put-in-Bay, Keats in Rome, The Death of Francisco Franco, Water Follies, Music and Exile, Catalogue of Bourgeois Objects, Signs and Certainties,* and *New Poems.*

Deborah A. Morrison holds an Honours B.A. Social Sciences from McMaster University, and has undergone extensive research in eastern and western thought within the framework of contemporary and comparative studies. She has achieved M.A. designation together with certification in Counseling Science, from the Counselor Training Institute, Vancouver, B.C., as recognized by the A.A.M.F.T., American Association of Marriage and Family Therapists. She is an internationally recognized author of poetry, fiction, and nonfiction books. Deborah's work brings inspiration and hope through the healing power of the written word. Deborah's first published poetry book, *Mystical Poetry,* was nominated and short listed for the Hamilton Literary Council Arts Award. Deborah is a proud mother and grandmother who encourages compassion and creativity in her family. To learn more about her and her inspirational books see: www.DeborahaMorrison.com

By Deborah A. Morrison: POETRY: *Mystical Poetry* (Manor House Publishing, 2000); PROSE: *Finding Your Center: Explorations in Philosophy, New Physics and Eastern Mysticism* (Cygnet Publications, 2017), *WISE WORDS: Insightful Reflections* (Manor House Publishing, 2012), *In The Garden: Where Inspiration Grows* (Manor House Publishing, 2009), *The Law of Attraction: Making it Work For You* (Manor House Publishing, 2009), and *NEXUS* (Manor House Publishing, 2006).

Colin Morton is an Ottawa writer. Colin has twice won the Archibald Lampman Award for Poetry. He also published a novel and coproduced an award-winning animated film. He has been a teacher, editor, small press publisher, performance poet, essayist, reviewer, web editor, writer-in-residence at Connecticut College and Concordia College (Minnesota), vice-president of the League of Canadian Poets, and a director of Ottawa's Tree Readings Series.

By Colin Morton: POETRY: *Winds and Strings* (BuschekBooks, 2013), *The Hundred Cuts: Sitting Bull and the Major* (BuschekBooks, 2009), *The Local Cluster* (Pecan Grove Press, 2008), *The Cabbage of Paradise: The Merzbook and other poems* (Seraphim Editions, 2007), *Dance, Misery* (Seraphim Editions, 2003), *Coastlines of the Archipelago* (BuschekBooks, 2000), *Coastlines* (above/ground press, 1999), *Mood Indigo* (Grove Avenue Press, 1996), *How to Be Born Again* (Quarry Press, 1991), *Musical Ride* (Clarion Press, 1990), *The Merzbook: Kurt Schwitters Poems* (Quarry Press, 1987), *Two Decades* (Ouroboros, 1987), *North/South:*

Performance Scores for One to Seven Voices (Underwhich Editions, 1987), *Wordmusic* (First Draft, 1986), *This Won't Last Forever* (Longspoon Press, 1985), *The Scream: First Draft, third annual group show* (Ouroboros, 1984), *Printed Matter* (Sidereal Press, 1982), and *In Transit* (Thistledown Press, 1981); NOVEL: *Oceans Apart* (Quarry Press, 1995).

Marion Mutala has a master's degree in educational administration and taught for 30 years. With a passion for the arts, she loves to write, sing, and play guitar, travel and read. Marion is the author of the bestselling and award-winning children's book trilogy, *Baba's Babushka: A Magical Ukrainian Christmas, Baba's Babushka: A Magical Ukrainian Easter,* and *Baba's Babushka: A Magical Ukrainian Wedding.* Her fourth book, *Grateful* was published in 2014. Her fifth book, *The Time for Peace is Now* published in 2015, and her debut poetry collection, *Ukrainian Daughter's Dance*, was published in 2016. *The Mechanic's Wife*, her first murder mystery, was released in 2016, and *More Baba's Please!*, her 6th children's book, was released 2017. *Kohkum's Babushka: A Magical Metis / Ukrainian Tale* is her 9th book, released 2017. She has two books forthcoming: *More Delightful Didos!* and *My Dearest Dido* — a book about the Ukrainian genocide — the Holodomor. Visit her website at: www.babasbabushka.ca

By Marion Mutlal: *Ukrainian Daughter's Dance* (2016).

Lois Nantais is a Psychology Professor at Lambton College and has taught courses in philosophy, sociology, psychology and interpersonal communication. With a Master's Degree in Moral Psychology, Nantais established and coordinates the Centre for Academic Integrity (CAI) at Lambton College, a peer-based student initiative supporting a culture of ethical leadership in the academic context. Nantais understands moral development as a facet of self-understanding, using narrative as an important approach for personal development. Nantais, a poet with two chapbooks, *of tender days* and *The Heaviness of Rain*, is co-editing an anthology of student poetry and prose from Lambton College called *Speak Up/Speak Out*. Nantais has published her work in *Ascent Aspirations*, *Harpweaver*, and *Room Magazine*. She is a member of After Hours Poets and lives in the Lambton County countryside with her husband and very poetic cat.

By Lois Nantais: *of tender days* and *The Heaviness of Rain*.

Shane Neilson is a poet, physician, and critic from New Brunswick. He is currently a Vanier Scholar researching the representations of pain in Canadian literature at McMaster University. Upon publishing *Dysphoria* with PQL last year, Shane completed his poetic affect trilogy. In 2017, he won the *Walrus Poetry Prize* and published in *Poetry Magazine*. He is the editor of Victoria-based Frog Hollow Press and is an associate editor at *Hamilton Arts & Letters Magazine*.

By Shane Neilson: POETRY: *Dysphoria* (The Porcupine's Quill, 2017), *An Equally Uncharitable Wonderland* (Frog Hollow Press, 2017), *New Brunswick* (Serif of Nottingham Press, 2016), *On Shaving* (The Porcupine's Quill, 2015), *The Manifesto of Fervourism* (Kelowna: Ryga Press, 2015), *On Shaving Off His Face* (Alfred Gustav Press, 2014), *We need our names* (Anstruther Press, 2014), *Out of the Mouth* (Thee Hellbox Press, 2014), *Able Physiologists Discuss Grief Musculatures* (Jackpine Press, 2014), *Love in a Czech Winter* (Cactus Press, 2011), *Complete Physical* (The Porcupine's Quill, 2010), *Field Hospital: The Last Writings of John McCrae* (Jackpine Press, 2010), *Elision: The Milton Acorn Poems* (Alfred Gustav Press, 2010), *Meniscus* (Biblioasis Press, 2009), *Seized* (Cubicle Press, 2004), and *The Beaten-Down Elegies* (Frog Hollow Press, 2003); PROSE: *Will* (Enfield and Wizenty Press, 2013), *Gunmetal Blue* (Palimpsest Press, 2011), and *Call Me Doctor* (Pottersfield Press, 2006).

Diane Attwell Palfrey is a poet/prose writer and a member of several poetry organizations. Her poetry collection *Intake of Glass* was published in 2013. Diane has work published in numerous anthologies and she regularly participates in publications/contests throughout Canada and the United States.

By Diane Attwell Palfrey: *Intake of Glass* (2013).

Brian Palmu is a poet and reviewer on the Sunshine Coast, British Columbia. Previous work has appeared in *Canadian Notes & Queries, Maisonneuve, subTerrain, Quills,* and *The Steel Chisel*. His debut poetry chapbook, *Sunset Mathematics,* was published by Frog Hollow Press in 2017.

By Brian Palmu: *Sunset Mathematics* (Frog Hollow Press, 2017).

Deborah Panko taught English in Toronto high schools, retiring in Cobourg on the north shore of Lake Ontario where she watches birds, rides her bike, practices the yogic Tibetan Rites, and cooks healthy dinners with her partner, Michael. Along with the wealth of local arts, she enjoys reading the classics with her book club and, when inspired, has a go at the piano. In 2008, Hidden Brook Press published her first book of poetry, *Somewhat Elsewhere*, then in 2010 *From O to Snow*, a book of poems shared with Kate Marshall Flaherty and Donna Langevin. In 2013, Crow-Magnon published *Photograph Do Not Bend/Poems Not For Pretend*, a book of her poetry and photographs by her late husband, Ron Cole, a photojournalist. These were followed by another book of poetry, *Blueprint,* in 2014 and a 'mythical' memoir/satire, *Full-Bodied,* in 2017. Contact: crow.magnon.media@gmail.com

By Deborah Panko: *Full-Bodied* (2017), *Blueprint* (2014), *Photograph Do Not Bend/Poems Not For Pretend* (Crow-Magnon, 2013), and *Somewhat Elsewhere* (Hidden Brook Press, 2008).

Chris Pannell has published six books of poetry. His collection *A Nervous City* (released in 2013) won the Kerry Schooley Book Award from the Hamilton Arts Council. In 2010, his book *Drive* won the Acorn-Plantos People's Poetry Prize and the Arts Hamilton Poetry Book of the Year. From 1993 to 2005 he ran the *new writing workshop* at Hamilton Artists Inc. and published two anthologies of work by that group. He is a former treasurer and board member for the gritLIT Writers Festival and a former DARTS bus driver. He has been involved with the Lit Live reading series for more than ten years. He is the former editor of *The Oxfordian*, the annual journal of the Shakespeare Oxford Fellowship based in Massachusetts. His latest book of poetry — *Love, Despite the Ache* — won the 2017 Literary Award for Poetry, from the Hamilton Arts Council (Ontario).

By Chris Pannell: *Love, Despite the Ache* (Hamilton, Ontario: Wolsak and Wynn, 2016), *A Nervous City* (Hamilton, Ontario: Wolsak and Wynn, 2013), *Everything Comes from Above* (Alfred Gustav Press, 2011), *Drive* (Hamilton, Ontario: Wolsak and Wynn, 2009), *Under Old Stars* (Seraphim Editions, 2003), and *Sorry I Spent Your Poem* (watershedBooks, 1999).

Gianna Patriarca is a graduate of York University, an award-winning author of 8 books of poetry, one children's book, and a collection of short fiction *All My Fallen Angelas*, inspired by the lives of Italian/Canadian women in Toronto. Her writing is extensively anthologized and appears on the course list of universities in Italy, Canada, and the USA. Gianna's writing has been adapted for Canada Stage at the Berkley Street Theater, CBC radio drama, and appears in numerous documentaries. Her first book *Italian Women and Other Tragedies* is in its 4th printing and is translated into Italian. Gianna has presented her work in many cities in Italy and North America and has been invited to read her work at Yale, Purdue, the University of Toronto, York University, Trent, Western, Paterson N.J., University of Bologna, and the University of Naples Orientale. She writes in English, Italian, and in her first language the "ciociaro" dialect. She is currently working on a novel, *The Sicilian's Bride*, and a new poetry collection, *Time to be Old*.

By Gianna Patriarca: POETRY: *Too Much Love* (Toronto: Quattro Books, 2012), *Donne Italiane ed Altre Tragedie* (Toronto: Lyricalmyrical, 2009), *My Etruscan Face* (Toronto: Quattro Books, 2007), *What My Arms Can Carry* (Toronto: Guernica Editions, 2003), *The Invisible Woman* (Toronto: Lyricalmyrical, 2001), *Ciao Baby* (Toronto: Guernica Editions, 1999), *Daughters for Sale* (Toronto: Guernica Editions, 1997), and *Italian Women and Other Tragedies* (Toronto: Guernica Editions, 1994); SHORT STORIES: *All My Fallen Angelas* (Inanna Publications, 2016); CHILDREN'S BOOK: *Nonna and the Girls Next Door* (Toronto: Lyricalmyrical, 2002).

Nolan Natasha Pike is a queer and trans writer living in Halifax, Nova Scotia. His poems have appeared in *The Puritan, Event,* and *Plenitude*. He has been short-listed for the *Geist* postcard contest, *Room* magazine's poetry contest, the Atlantic Writing Competition, and has been long-listed for the CBC poetry prize.

By Nolan Natasha Pike: *Batting Practice* (Paisley Press, 2012).

Stella Mazur Preda is a resident of Waterdown, Ontario. She is owner and publisher of Serengeti Press, a small press publishing company, located in the Hamilton area. Since its opening in 2003, Serengeti Press has published 43 Canadian books. (Serengeti Press is now temporarily on hiatus.) Stella Mazur Preda has been published in numerous Canadian anthologies and some U.S., most notable was the purchase of her poem "My Mother's Kitchen" by Penguin Books, New York. Stella has released four previous books, *Butterfly Dreams* (Serengeti Press, 2003); *Witness, Anthology of Poetry* (Serengeti Press, 2004), edited by John B. Lee; *From Rainbow Bridge to Catnip Fields* (chapbook, Serengeti Press, 2007); *The Fourth Dimension* (Serengeti Press, 2012). She is a current member of Tower Poetry Society and The Ontario Poetry Society. Stella is currently working on her third book, *Tapestry*, based on the life of her aunt and written completely in poetic form. *Tapestry* will be released in the Fall of 2018.

By Stella Mazur Preda: *The Fourth Dimension* (Serengeti Press, 2012), *From Rainbow Bridge to Catnip Fields* (Serengeti Press, 2007), and *Butterfly Dreams* (Serengeti Press, 2003).

Robert Priest is the author of fourteen books of poetry, three plays, four novels, lots of musical CDs, and one hit song. His words have been debated in the legislature, posted in the Transit system, quoted in the *Farmer's Almanac*, and sung on *Sesame Street*. His 2008 book, *Reading the Bible Backwards*, peaked at number two on the Canadian poetry charts. *Rosa Rose*, a book of children's verse in praise of inspirational figures, was a book of honour in the Lion And the Unicorn Prize of excellence in Children's Literature. A new book of children's poems, *The Wolf is Back*, has just come out with Wolsak & Wynn, coinciding with his latest recording *BAAM!*, which is available on CD baby and for a limited time on Youtube at http://poempainter.com/x

By Robert Priest: POETRY: *The Wolf is Back* (Wolsak & Wynn, 2017), *Previously Feared Darkness* (ECW, 2014), *Rosa Rose* (Wolsak & Wynn, 2013), *Reading the Bible Backwards* (ECW, 2008), *How to Swallow a Pig: Collected Prose Poems* (2004), *Blue Pryamids: Selected Poems* (ECW, 2002), *Resurrection in the Cartoon* (ECW, 1997), *A Terrible Case of the Stars* (Penguin, 1994), *Daysongs Nightsongs* (Groundwood, 1993), *The Mad Hand* (Coach House Press, 1988), *The Ruby Hat* (Aya Press, 1985), *The Man who broke out of the Letter X* (Coach House Press, 1984), *Sadness of Spacemen* (Dreadnaught Press, 1980), and *The Visible Man* (Unfinished Monument Press, 1979); FICTION: *Missing Piece* (Dundurn Press, 2017), *Second Kiss* (Dundurn Press, 2015), *The Paper Sword* (Dundurn Press, 2013), *The Ballad of the Blue*

Bonnet (Groundwood, 1994), *Knights of the Endless Day* (Viking, 1993), and *The Short Hockey Career of Amazing Jany* (Aya Press, 1985).

Brian Purdy was born in Canada in 1948. He is married to Katie Pataki, resides in Halifax, Nova Scotia, does not own an automobile, and frequently holds the challenge table all night at his local watering hole against all comers. Besides pool he also enjoys cycling and watercolour sketching. He continues to write new song lyrics and poems into his seventieth year. Later in 2018, he hopes to see a new volume of poems in print. This will be titled *from higher ground*. He is the author of several books of poems and one book of short stories.

By Brian Purdy: POETRY: *To Feed the Sun* (Three Trees Press), *Strips* (Letters Bookshop Press), and *Black Ink Portraits* (Big Pond Rumors Press); PROSE: *Interloper* (Three Trees Press) and *A Poet's Garden* (Big Pond Rumors Press).

Kathy Robertson's creative writing, essays, and poetry have appeared in a number of journals and anthologies including *Crannóg Literary Journal, Taj Mahal Review, The Avocet, The Ontario Poetry Society*, and *Tower Poetry*. She was the essay winner in The Elora Writers' Festival 2017 Contest for her work entitled "My Canadian Moment." Five of her poems were published in an anthology of Canadian writers entitled *Simply Because We are Canadians*, in honor of Canada's 150th birthday. She was a presenter at the Bluewater Reading Series, and a panelist at a literary event discussing the topic "From Monologue to Dialogue" with keynote speaker John Greenwood. She received her B.Ed. from the University of Western Ontario. Her B.A. was attained at Wilfrid Laurier University, Waterloo, where she graduated with an English major and a double minor in History/Psychology. She is a member of The Ontario Poetry Society, Tower Poetry Society, and the Cambridge Writers' Collective. She lives in Kitchener, Ontario with her husband Norm and enjoys theater, lecture series, bridge, and lawn bowling.

By Kathy Robertson: *Poetic Ponderings, a reflective tapestry of life's joys and sorrows.*

Denis Robillard is a 51 year old poet and educator born in Northern Ontario. He now resides with his wife and children in Windsor, Ontario. His poetic works have appeared in over 300 magazines, journals, and books in Canada, England, Scotland, and the United States. In 2005 his collection *Zuk, Zuk, Zuk* was published in New York. Recent publications include *Ristau* (Kentucky), *Rampike* (Canada), *The Ekphrastic Review* (Canada), *The Windsor Review*, and *LUMMOX* (California). He is the past winner of the Ted Plantos Poetry Award in 2015 and winner of the Cranberry Tree Press Award for his book, *The History of Water*. Black Moss Press will publish his next full volume of poems called *Ask the River* in Spring 2018.

By Denis Robillard: *Ask the River* (Windsor, Ontario: Black Moss, 2018), *The History of Water*, and *Zuk, Zuk, Zuk*.

Kate Rogers' new poetry collection, *Out of Place*, debuted with Aeolus House/Quattro Books) in Toronto in 2017. During the autumn of 2017, *Out of Place* also launched in Hong Kong, at the Singapore Writers Festival and the Asia Pacific Writers and Translators conference in Bali, Indonesia. Kate was shortlisted for the *Montreal International Poetry Prize* in July 2017. She has poetry forthcoming in the anthology, *Catherines, the Great* (Oolichan). Her work has appeared in *Twin Cities Cinema (Hong Kong-Singapore), Juniper, Quixotica, Poems East of La Mancha, Of Zoos, The Guardian, Eastlit, Asia Literary Review, Cha: an Asian Literary Journal, Morel, The Goose: a journal of Arts, Environment and Culture* (Wilfred Laurier University), *Kyoto Journal, ASIATIC: the Journal of the International Islamic University of Malaysia, Many Mountains Moving, Orbis International*, among others. She lectures in literature and media studies at the Community College of City University in Hong Kong.

By Kate Rogers: *Out of Place* (Aeolus House/Quattro Books, 2017), *Foreign Skin* (Aeolus House, 2015), *City of Stairs* (Haven Books, 2012), and *Painting the Borrowed House* (Proverse Publishing, 2008).

Linda Rogers, Past President of the League of Canadian Poets, Victoria Poet Laureate, and Canadian People's Poet publishes poetry, children's books, adult fiction, short fiction, lyrics, and journalism. She has won the Bridport, Kenney Cardiff, Acorn-Rukeyser, Livesay, Leacock, MacEwan, and National Poetry Awards. Her current titles are *Bozuk,* a Turkish memoir, *Crow Jazz*, short stories, and *Hello!Wiksas!,* illustrated by Chief Rande Cook, for children. Rogers often collaborates with her husband, blues mandolinist Rick van Krugel.

By Linda Rogers: POETRY: *Homing* (Ekstasis Editions, 2012), *Muscle Memory* (Ekstasis Editions, 2009), *The Bursting Test* (Guernica Editions, 2002), *Rehearsing the Miracle* (Poppy Press fine art edition, 2001), *Grief Sits Down* (Canadian Poetry Association, Shaunt Basmajian Award, 2000), *The Saning* (Sono Nis, 1999), *Picking the Stones* (Hamilton, Ontario: Unfinished Monument Press, Acorn-Ruckeyser Award, 1998), *Heaven Cake* (Sono Nis, 1997), *Love in the Rainforest: selected poems* (Exile, 1995), *Hard Candy* (Sono Nis, 1994), *The Magic Flute* (The Porcupine's Quill, 1988), and *Woman at Mile Zero* (Oolichan, 1998); FICTION: *Bozuk* (Exile, 2016), *Tempo Rubato* (2015), *The Empress Letters* (Cormorant Books, 2007), *Friday Water* (Cormorant Books, 2003), *Say My Name, the memoirs of Charlie Louie* (Ekstasis Editions, 2000), and *The Half Life of Radium* (Sono Nis, 1994); NON-FICTION: *bill bissett, essays on his work* (Guernica Editions, 2002), *Al Purdy, essays on his work* (Guernica Editions, 2002), *PK Page, essays on her work* (Guernica Editions, 2001), and *The Broad Canvas — portraits of women artists* (Sono Nis, 1999); FOR CHILDREN: *Molly Brown is Not a Clown* (Ronsdale, 1995), *Frankie Zapper and the Disappearing Teacher* (Ronsdale, 1994), *Brown Bag Blues* (Studio 123, 1990), and *Worm Sandwich* (Sono Nis, 1987).

Karen Shenfeld has published three books with Guernica Editions: *The Law of Return* (1999), which won the Canadian Jewish Book Award for Poetry in 2001, *The Fertile Crescent* (2005), and *My Father's Hands Spoke in Yiddish* (2010). Her poetry has also appeared in journals and anthologies published in Canada, the U.S., England, South Africa, and Bangladesh. It has been featured on Canada's CBC Radio and CKLN, and on "39 Dover Street", a British short-wave radio programme. Shenfeld has been awarded Canada, Ontario, and Toronto Arts Council Grants, and she has been long-listed for a ReLit Award. In 2010 and 2015, she travelled to Mexico to participate in the annual Festival Internacional Literario de Linares. She has also given readings in Canada, the U.S., England, and South Africa. As well, Shenfeld has brought her poetic sensibility to the writing of magazine stories and to filmmaking. Her personal documentaries include: *Il Giardino, The Gardens of Little Italy* (2007) and *Maggie & Merly* (2017).

By Karen Shenfeld: *My Father's Hands Spoke in Yiddish* (Guernica Editions, 2010), *The Fertile Crescent* (Guernica Editions, 2005), and *The Law of Return* (Guernica Editions, 1999).

Glen Sorestad is a Saskatoon poet whose work has been published widely throughout North America and in various other countries. His poems have appeared in over 70 anthologies and have been translated into eight languages. His most recent books of poetry include *Hazards of Eden: Poems from the Southwest* (Lamar University Press, 2015) and *Water and Rock* (Lea County Museum Press, 2017). Sorestad was the first provincially appointed poet laureate, Saskatchewan's first Poet Laureate in 2000, and was named a Member of the Order of Canada in 2010.

By Glan Sorestad: *Water and Rock: Fish and Friends in the Boreal North*, with Jim Harris (LCM Press, 2017), *Hazards of Eden: Poems from the Southwest* (Lamar University Press, 2015), *Along Okema Road* (Rubicon Press, 2013), *A Thief of Impeccable Taste* (Sandcrab Books, 2011), *What We Miss* (Thistledown Press, 2010), *Road Apples* (Rubicon Press, 2009), *Language of Horse* (Coracle Press, 2007), *Halo of Morning* (Leaf Press, 2006), *Blood & Bone, Ice & Stone* (Thistledown Press, 2005), *Grasses & Gravestones* (Smoky Peace Press, 2003), *Dreaming My Grandfather's Dreams* (Frog Hollow Press, 2002), *Leaving Holds Me Here: Selected Poems 1975-2000* (Thistledown Press, 2001), *Today I Belong to Agnes* (Ekstasis Editions, 2000), *Icons of Flesh* (Ekstasis Editions, 1998), *Birchbark Meditations* (Writers on the Plains, 1996), *Jan Lake Sharing*, with Jim Harris (Privately printed, 1993), *West Into Night* (Thistledown Press, 1991), *Air Canada Owls* (Nightwood Editions, 1990), *Stalking Place: Poems Across Borders*, with Jim Harris and Peter Christensen (Hawk Press, 1988), *Hold the Rain in Your Hands: Poems New and*

Selected (Coteau Books, 1985), *Jan Lake Poems* (Harbour Publishing, 1984), *Ancestral Dances* (Thistledown Press, 1979), *Pear Seeds in My Mouth* (Sesame Press, 1977), *Prairie Pub Poems* (Thistledown Press 1976), *Wind Songs* (Thistledown Press, 1975), and *Prairie Pub Poems* (Anak Press, 1973).

Ken Stange was an American-born (b. Chicago, 1946) Canadian writer, editor, visual artist, and professor at Nipissing University, who lived and worked in North Bay, Ontario, from 1971 until his death in 2016. He married in 1966, graduated from Loyola University in 1968 and, in protest against the Vietnam War, with his wife immigrated to Canada, became citizens, and had two children. From the early '70s until his retirement, Stange taught Psychology at Nipissing University and, in that time, with the support of the Canada Council and the Ontario Arts Council, he published 23 major works of poetry, prose, and digital art as well as hundreds of poems, reviews, and essays in literary periodicals, magazines, and major poetry anthologies in Canada and internationally. Also in the early '70s, he founded and edited the small literary periodical, *Nebula*, which ran until 1982, and then in 2008, Two Cultures Press, a small literary publishing house and online presence, publishing many of his later works as well as making earlier works available electronically for the first time.

By Ken Stange: POETRY: *The Sad Science of Love* (Two Cultures Press, 2010), *Advice To Travellers* (Penumbra Press, 1994), *Nocturnal Rhythms* (Penumbra Press, 1979), *Love Is a Grave* (Nebula Press, 1978), *Portraits In The Mirror* (Nebula Press, 1978), *Revenging Language* (Fiddlehead Books, 1976), and *Wolf Cycle* (Nebula Press, 1974); POETRY & PROSE: *Bourgeois Pleasures* (Quarry Press, 1984) and *Cold Pigging Poetics* (York Publishing, 1981); FICTION: *God When He's Drunk* (Two Cultures Press, 2012), *More Than Ample* (Two Cultures Press, 2009), and *Bushed* (York Publishing, 1979); NON-FICTION: *Chicago Days: Growing Up Absurd On The South Side* (Two Cultures Press, 2016), *The Secret Agents: Going Where There Be Dragons* (Two Cultures Press, 2014), *The Secret Agents: Looking Through A Glass Darkly* (Two Cultures Press, 2014), *The Secret Agents: The Parting Of The Waters* (Two Cultures Press, 2014), *Explaining Canada: A Primer For Yanks* (Two Cultures Press, 2014), *Going Home: Cycling Through The Heart Of America* (Two Cultures Press, 2014), and *These Proses A Problem Or Two* (Two Cultures Press, 2008); OTHER: *Art's In The Head, Not The Hand* (Two Cultures Press, 2015), *Embracing The Moon* (Two Cultures Press, 2013), *Colonization Of A Cold Planet* (Two Cultures Press, 2008), and *A Smoother Pebble, A Prettier Shell* (Penumbra Press, 1996).

J.J. Steinfeld is a fiction writer, poet, and playwright who lives on Prince Edward Island, where he is patiently waiting for Godot's arrival and a phone call from Kafka. While waiting, he has published eighteen books, including *Anton Chekhov Was Never in Charlottetown* (Stories, Gaspereau), *Would You Hide Me?* (Stories, Gaspereau), *An Affection for Precipices* (Poetry,

Serengeti), *Word Burials* (Novel and Stories, Crossing Chaos Enigmatic Ink), *Misshapenness* (Poetry, Ekstasis Editions), *Identity Dreams and Memory Sounds* (Poetry, Ekstasis Editions), *Madhouses in Heaven, Castles in Hell* (Stories, Ekstasis Editions), *An Unauthorized Biography of Being* (Stories, Ekstasis Editions), and *Absurdity, Woe Is Me, Glory Be* (Poetry, Guernica Editions). Over fifty of his one-act plays and a handful of full-length plays have been performed in Canada and the United States, including the full-length plays *The Franz Kafka Therapy Session*, *The Golden Age of Monsters*, and *A Television-Watching Artist*; and one-act plays *Godot's Leafless Tree, The Waiting Ends, The Entrance-or-Not Barroom,* and *In a Washroom of a Prestigious Art;* and the radio plays *In Becky's Name, The Professor's Ashes,* and *Diogenes' Lantern.*

By J.J. Steinfeld: POETRY: *Absurdity, Woe Is Me, Glory Be* (Guernica Editions, 2017), *Identity Dreams and Memory Sounds: Poetry New & Selected* (Ekstasis Editions, 2014), *A Fanciful Geography* (erbacce-press, 2010), *Misshapenness* (Ekstasis Editions, 2009), *Where War Finds You* (HMS Press, 2008), *An Affection for Precipices* (Serengeti Press, 2006), and *Existence Is a Hoax, a Woman in Fishnet Stockings Told Me When I Was Twenty* (Cubicle Press, 2003); FICTION: *An Unauthorized Biography of Being* (Ekstasis Editions, 2016), *Madhouses in Heaven, Castles in Hell* (Ekstasis Editions, 2015), *A Glass Shard and Memory* (Recliner Books, 2010), *Word Burials* (Crossing Chaos Enigmatic Ink, 2009), *Not a Second More, Not a Second Less* (Mercutio Press, 2005), *Would You Hide Me?* (Gaspereau Press, 2003), *Curiosity to Satisfy and Fear to Placate* (Mercutio Press, 2003), *Anton Chekhov Was Never in Charlottetown* (Gaspereau Press, 2000), *Should the Word Hell Be Capitalized?* (Gaspereau Press, 1999), *Disturbing Identities* (Ekstasis Editions, 1997), *Dancing at the Club Holocaust: Stories New & Selected* (Ragweed Press, 1993), *The Miraculous Hand and Other Stories* (Ragweed Press, 1991), *Unmapped Dreams* (Crossed Keys Publishing, 1989), *Forms of Captivity and Escape* (Thistledown Press, 1988), *Our Hero in the Cradle of Confederation* (Pottersfield Press, 1987), and *The Apostate's Tattoo* (Ragweed Press, 1983).

Dane Swan was born in Bermuda and is based in Toronto. A former slam poet, Swan's second poetry collection, *A Mingus Lullaby*, was short-listed for the 2017 Trillium Book Prize for Poetry. Recently branching into prose, his first short story collection was published in 2017, and the manuscript for his first novella, *Tuesday*, was a finalist in Grey Borders Books "Wanted Works" competition in 2016. Grey Borders published *Tuesday*, in the Spring of 2018. Currently editing an anthology of poetry and prose for Guernica Editions, Dane is also rumored to be in talks with an undisclosed publisher to run his own imprint.

By Dane Swan: *Tuesday* (Grey Borders, 2018), *He Doesn't Hurt People Anymore* (Dumagrad Books, 2017), *A Mingus Lullaby* (Guernica Editions, 2016), *Bending the Continuum* (Guernica Editions, 2011), *Narcotics//Flora* (Burning Effigy Press, 2009), and *Grey Clouds* (Self-published, 2005).

Lynn Tait is a Toronto-born award-winning poet and photographer, residing in Sarnia, Ontario. She has published poetry in major poetry magazines, journals, including, *Contemporary Verse 2, FreeFall, Windsor Review*, the *Literary Review of Canada*, and in over 90 anthologies including five annual Lummox anthologies. She has published a chapbook, *Breaking Away,* and co-authored a book, *Encompass I*. Her photography/digital images have appeared on the covers of seven poetry books. She is a member of The Ontario Poetry Society, the League of Canadian Poets, and is co-founder of the local poetry workshop, After Hours Poets.

By Lynn Tait: *Breaking Away* (Sarnia, Ontario: Wine&Cheese Press, 2002).

Jennifer Tan has received an honourable mention in the literary contest of the Eden Mills Writers' Festival in 2002 for her short story "Dirt on My Face". She has been published in local anthologies and by the *Hamilton Spectator* while serving on the Community Editorial Board from 2003 to 2005. In 2003 she attended a memorable writing workshop in Siena with Alistair MacLeod as her teacher. She is a committee member of Hamilton's monthly LitLive Literary Readings and a member of Tower Poetry Society, where she has served on the editorial board since 2011. Jennifer hosts LitChat, Hamilton's monthly literary salon. She received the 2016 Short Works Prize for Published Poetry for her poem "From Apples and Skulls". Her interests include running, dancing, gardening, painting, learning languages, travelling, and eating well.

Grace Vermeer was born in Mississippi in 1960 and grew up in Ohio, Pennsylvania, and Montana. She came to Canada as a student and has made it her home since 1982. Her poetry has received a number of awards including the Eleanor B. Mathews Award (SC4), the Lillian Kroll Prize for Creative Writing (Western University), and the Monica Ladell Award (Scarborough Arts). Her work has appeared in *Patterns, Big Art Book, Lummox,* and *Vallum*. She has three grown children and lives with her husband in Sarnia, Ontario.

Wendy Visser is an established poet and the author of two poetry collections: *Riding A Wooden Horse* (winner of the WRAC book award in 2007) and *This Side of Beyond*, and co-author with Becky D. Alexander of *haiku by two*. She was one of eight Canadian poets featured in the anthology, *Quern*, and a contributor in the recently published, *Simply Because We Are Canadian*, the Cambridge Writers Collective's project to celebrate Canada's sesquicentennial. A former recipient of the Bernice Adams Memorial Award for her involvement in Communications/literary Arts, Wendy continues to promote the arts in Cambridge. Wendy is a member of the Cambridge Writers Collective, the Ontario Poetry Society, Tower Poetry, and Poets Roundtable Arkansas. She is currently working on two new manuscripts and when not writing, she divides her literary interests between contest judging, workshop facilitating, editing and proofreading.

By Wendy Visser: *This Side of Beyond* (Craigleigh Press, 2011), *haiku by two* (Craigleigh Press, 2007), and *Riding A Wooden Horse* (Craigleigh Press, 2005).

Bruce Whiteman is a poet and book reviewer. He has lived in Montreal, Hamilton, the American Midwest, and Los Angeles, and now lives in Toronto. He teaches part-time at the University of Toronto and is the Poet-in-Residence at Scattergood Friends School in West Branch, Iowa. His reviews have appeared widely in such places as *Canadian Notes & Queries, Quill & Quire*, the *Toronto Star, The Antigonish Review*, the *Los Angeles Review of Books, The Hudson Review, Pleiades*, and elsewhere. His most recent poetry collections are *Intimate Letters* (ECW Press, 2014) and *Tablature* (McGill-Queen's University Press, 2015). *Intimate Letters* forms the seventh book of his long poem, *The Invisible World Is in Decline*.

By Bruce Whiteman: POETRY: *Tablature* (McGill-Queen's University Press, 2015), *Intimate Letters: The Invisible World Is in Decline, Book VII* (ECW Press, 2014), *The Invisible World Is in Decline, Books I-VI* (ECW Press, 2006), *Tristia* (Vero Press, 2002), *XXIV Love Poems* (Ninja Press, 2002), *The Invisible World Is in Decline, Book V* (ECW Press, 2000), *The Forger Contemplates Rossetti* (Lyceum Press, 2000), *Visible Stars: New and Selected Poems* (The Muses' Company, 1995), *Zukofsky Impromptus* (Sin Tax, 1995), *Polyphonic Windows* (Poets & Painters Press, 1993), *The Invisible World Is in Decline, Books II-IV* (Coach House Press, 1989), *En avoir fini avec le corps seul* (La Presse des Poètes et des Peintres d'Outre-Mer, 1987), *A Nature Murder* (Poets & Painters Press, 1985), *Recesses in the Heart: The Thera Poems* (blewointmentpress, 1984), *The Invisible World Is in Decline* (Coach House Press, 1984), *The Cold Engineering of the World* (League of Canadian Poets, 1983), *The Thera Poems* (Warren House Press, 1982), *10 Lessons in Autobiography* (Gryphon Press, 1981), *Inventions* (Three Trees Press, 1979), *The Sun At Your Thighs, The Moon At Your Lips* (Piraeus Press, 1978), and *12 Poems, 12 Drawings* (Poets & Painters Press, 1978); TRANSLATION: Tiberianus. *Pervigilium Veneris* (Russell Maret, 2009), Catullus. *LXXXV/CV: Two Poems in Five Essays* (Lyceum Press, 2006), and François Charron. *After 10,000 Years, Desire: Selected Recent Poems* (ECW Press, 1995); CULTURAL HISTORY: *Francis Jammes: On the Life & Work of a Modern Master* (Pleiades Press, 2014), *The World from Here: Treasures of the Great Libraries of Los Angeles* (UCLA Armand Hammer Museum, 2001), *J.E.H. Macdonald* (Quarry Press, 1995), *Lasting Impressions: A Short History of English Publishing in Quebec* (Véhicule Press, 1994), *The Letters of John Sutherland, 1942-1956* (ECW Press, 1992), *Raymond Souster and His Works* (ECW Press, 1985), *Raymond Souster: A Descriptive Bibliography* (Oberon Press, 1984), *A Literary Friendship: The Correspondence of Ralph Gustafson and W.W.E. Ross* (ECW Press, 1984), and *Leonard Cohen: An Annotated Bibliography* (ECW Press, 1980).

Elana Wolff is a Toronto-based writer, editor, translator, photographer, designer, and facilitator of social art courses. Her poetry and prose have appeared in Canadian and international publications and have garnered awards. Her fifth solo collection of poetry, *Everything Reminds You of Something Else*, was released in 2017 with Guernica Editions. Her essay, "Paging Kafka's Elegist," won *The New Quarterly* 2015 Edna Staebler Personal Essay Contest and is included in Tightrope Books *Best Canadian Essays 2016*. "Kafka at the Cemetery" was short listed for *The Malahat Review* 2016 Constance Rooke Prize for Creative Non-fiction. Elana's newest Kafka-quest essays are in current issues of *New Madrid*, journal of contemporary literary, *Humber Literary Review*, and *Wanderlust Journal*.

By Elana Wolff: *Everything Reminds You of Something Else* (Guernica Editions, 2017), *You Will Still Have Birds: a conversation in poems with Susie Berg* (Lyricalmyrical, 2015), *Poems and Songs of Love* by Georg Mordechai Langer, translated from the Hebrew with Menachem Wolff (Guernica Editions, 2014), *Helleborus & Alchémille* — a bilingual collection of poems selected from *Birdheart*, *Mask*, *You Speak to Me in Trees*, and *Startled Night*; translation by Stéphanie Roesler (Éditions du Noroît, 2013), *Startled Night* (Guernica Editions, 2011), *Implicate Me: Short Essays on Reading Contemporary Poems* (Guernica Editions, 2010), *Slow Dancing: Creativity and Illness*, with Malca Litovitz (Guernica Editions, 2008), *You Speak to Me in Trees* (Guernica Editions, 2006), *Mask* (Guernica Editions, 2003), and *Birdheart* (Guernica Editions, 2001).

Jan Wood loves writing, teaching, and living in Northern Saskatchewan. She is a member of the The Ontario Poetry Society and the Saskatchewan Writer's Guild. She is a juried member of the Saskatchewan Craft Council in fiber arts and creates hand-made journals from repurposed leathers. She has over 250 poems, short stories, and non-fiction articles printed in a variety of anthologies and magazines. Three times her poems were chosen as first place winners at the Canadian Word Guild Awards. She was Poet Laureate for utmostchristianwriters.com for 2 years and wrote the poetry section for *Inscribe* magazine (2016-2017). Her book of poetry, *Love is not Anonymous*, was published by Thistledown Press in 2015.

By Jan Wood: *Love is not Anonymous* (Thistledown Press, 2015).

Ed Woods was born in Toronto and now lives in Dundas, Ontario. While on surgical recovery from his tanker truck collision, discovered a poetry workshop and was encouraged by participants to expand upon employment and observations of life. Life as a pilot, pipeline construction, electronics, transportation, casino work, and sciences is often referred to as Industrial Poetry. In a effort to entertain as well as give a personal view or statement or opinion, he tries to find a different flow of a poem from the serious to comedic twist. Ed has self-published chapbooks and creative writing in many anthologies and is a member of Tower Poetry Society, The Ontario Poetry Society, World Poetry Group, and Hamilton Artists and Writers.

By Ed Woods: POETRY: *Haiku One*, *Haiku Two*, *Poetry and other unfortunate non-fiction*, *The Casino Shuttle*, *Poems One*, *Poems Two*, *Poems Three*, *Poems Four*, and *Survival*; FICTION: *Short Stories*. All from Frozen Foot Publishers.

Anna Yin was Mississauga's first Poet Laureate. She has published four poetry collections. Anna won the 2005 Ted Plantos Memorial Award, the 2010/2014 MARTY Awards, the 2013 Chinese Professionals Association of Canada Professional Achievement Award, and the 2016/2017 West Chester University Poetry Conference scholarships. She has been interviewed by CBC radio, TalentVision TV, Rogers TV, etc. Her poem: "My Accent" was selected for 2017 National Poetry Month's Pocket Poem and "Still Life" was part of the Poetry in Transit project featured on buses across Canada in 2013. Her poetry has also appeared on *Arc Poetry Magazine*, *The New York Times*, *China Daily*, CBC Radio, *World Journal*, *Literary Review of Canada*, etc. She has received three grants from the Ontario Art Council for her poetry projects. Her website: annapoetry.com

By Anna Yin: *Nightlights* (Black Moss Press, 2017), *Seven Nights with the Chinese Zodiac* (Black Moss Press, 2015), *Inhaling the Silence* (Mosaic Press 2013), and *Wings Toward Sunlight* (Mosaic Press, 2011).

www.ingramcontent.com/pod-product-compliance
Lightning Source LLC
Chambersburg PA
CBHW080430230426
43662CB00015B/2230